Catch of the Day

Catch of the Day

A FISH COOKBOOK

Carol Cutler

and the Editors of
Consumer Reports Books

CONSUMER REPORTS BOOKS
A Division of Consumers Union   *Yonkers, New York*

Copyright © 1990 by Carol Cutler
Published by Consumers Union of United States, Inc., Yonkers,
New York 10703.
Library of Congress Cataloging-in-Publication Data
Cutler, Carol.
Catch of the day: a fish cookbook / Carol Cutler and the editors
of Consumer Reports Books.
p.   cm.
ISBN 0–89043–285–6
ISBN 0–89043–341–0 (HC)
1. Cookery (Seafood)   I. Consumer Reports Books.   II.
Title.
TX747.C88   1989
641.6'92 — dc20
89–22222
CIP

Book design and composition by The Sarabande Press
Drawings by Mimi Harrison
Second printing, August 1995
Manufactured in the United States of America

To BJ, the salt of the earth

Contents

Five

PASTAS AND RISOTTOS

Six
PIZZAS AND PIES

Seven
SALADS

Catch of the Day

Introduction

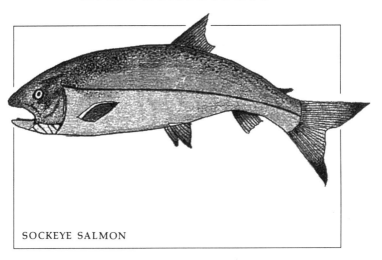

SOCKEYE SALMON

Fish is a unique food—it combines great taste with the added bonus of being low in fat and calories. It is this happy pairing that surely accounts for the current boom in seafood sales, both at the retail level and in restaurants all over the country.

As far as taste is concerned, I have favored fish over meat for as long as I can remember. Even in its more exotic forms, seafood has always intrigued me. Years ago, in a Spanish restaurant, I ordered a fish dish whose name was unfamiliar to me. The waiter tried to discourage me, to no avail. A while later he placed before me a dish of little gray blobs covered with a green topping. He stood by, expecting me to turn as green as the sauce. Much to his surprise, after one tentative taste, I proceeded to enjoy the meal with great gusto. This dish was my introduction to fish cheeks, those sweet little nuggets tucked away behind the gills of the fish. This experience taught me a lesson about the rewards of adventurous dining—fish come in all shapes and sizes, and each one (as well as its parts) has its own singular taste and textural appeal.

Today, as prices for traditional seafood spiral upward, more and more Americans are discovering the virtues of some types of fish that people all over the world have been enjoying for centuries. Mussels, of course, are no longer a rarity on menus or dinner tables. Squid is often served today in neighborhood restaurants, and catfish is no longer confined to southern home cooking. Monkfish was only offered in trendy restaurants a few years ago. Now, as its popularity increases, so does its price.

Indeed, all the fish in the sea (with very few exceptions) can find a place on the family dinner table, at formal and informal gatherings, on luncheon menus, and as picnic and barbecue fare.

A HEALTHY FOOD

The popularity of fish as a food source soared when researchers discovered that some fish is high in omega-3 polyunsaturated fatty acids. Omega-3 fatty acids typically remain liquid at extremely low temperatures. Studies have shown that these compounds alter the blood by making it less likely to coagulate or clot. It does this by making blood platelets less sticky and less likely to clump in the arteries, thus reducing the possibility of heart attacks and strokes. Generally, the colder the water and oilier the fish, the greater the omega-3 content.

Part of the recent research has served to retire former misconceptions about fish. Fatty fish, for example, were supposed to raise blood cholesterol. They don't. Studies have shown that experimental diets high in fish oil and salmon (a fatty fish) actually lower the level of cholesterol in the blood somewhat. Such diets also seem to dramatically reduce the blood level of triglycerides—fatty substances that are suspected of playing a role in coronary heart disease.

Of course, the term *fatty* as applied to fish is something of a misnomer. Compared with other food products, fish tend to be among the leaner food sources. Overall, oily fish—salmon, mackerel, bluefish, trout, sardines, herring, and the like—have only about one-fifth to one-half the average fat content of lean beef. Most shellfish, contrary to previous belief, are also low in fat. Recent analyses by the U.S. Department of Agriculture have shown that scallops, lobster, and shrimp are comparatively low in cholesterol.

Fish is also an important source of vitamins and minerals and is rich in iodine and generally low in sodium. Fish protein, moreover, is easier to digest than meat protein and is as good a source of essential amino acids as red meat.

SAFETY TIPS

Although eating fish in moderation is considered good for you, it is prudent to keep in mind possible health hazards from eating contaminated fish or shellfish.

Most problems arise when fish come from polluted waters. Unfortunately, at this time fish is not monitored by a mandatory federal inspection program. In fact, only a small number of federal and state programs exist to regulate the safety of fish, not nearly enough to cover all the fish and shellfish consumed in this country. Currently, there are proposals in Congress to establish such an inspection program, but to date this legislation has not been passed. How, then, can consumers protect themselves from the dangers of contaminated seafood? Here are some tips on buying, preparing, and cooking fish safely:

- Always purchase your fish or shellfish from a reliable, established source, preferably a store that has adequate storage and handling facilities and deals in high-quality products. Get to know your fishmonger, and don't hesitate to make inquiries about the origin and condition of the fish you are buying.
- Chill all fresh fish as soon as possible after purchase, and keep in the refrigerator until cooking time. Do not store unfrozen fish for more than three days, or shellfish for more than two. To prevent the threat of cross-contamination, avoid preparing other foods in the same area as raw fish or shellfish.
- Cook all fish thoroughly, until the flesh is opaque and flakes easily; avoid eating the skin, viscera, and fatty parts, where the toxic materials tend to concentrate. Always steam clams and other mollusks for at least four or five minutes, not just until the shells open.

- Eating raw shellfish puts you in a much higher risk category for bacteria or virus-caused illnesses. If shellfish come from an area where outbreaks of food poisoning are common, avoid eating them raw, if at all.
- Eating raw fish, such as preparations of Japanese sushi or sashimi, involves a risk mainly from an internal parasite known as the fish tapeworm. Although ocean fish usually are not a problem in this regard, lake fish and Alaskan salmon are sometimes infected. If you prepare raw fish yourself, stick to the ocean varieties.
- Vary the types of seafood in your diet. Commercially sold fish comes under federal regulations that strictly limit levels of mercury, pesticide residues, or other forms of toxic pollution, but too frequent consumption of one type of fish is not recommended. Large predators particularly, such as swordfish, tuna, red snapper, freshwater trout, or northern pike, are higher in the food chain, eat more, and live longer, and thus are more likely to have higher levels of pesticides, mercury, and other chemical contaminants.
- Freshwater fish, taken from major lakes or streams, are more likely to be contaminated by pollutants than ocean fish. (However, polluted conditions can exist in coastal waters near large cities.) Some fish, such as trout and catfish, are now available from aquafarms, where they are raised in cleaner, more controlled environments.
- If you eat fish that you catch yourself, avoid fishing in lakes or streams known to have pollution problems. Call your State Department of Health to get their latest bulletins on the possible contamination of local waters.

Despite the above cautions, the culinary and health benefits of including fish in your diet—several times a week—outweighs any risk. Overall, if you observe commonsense rules of purchase, sanitation, and preparation, you can reduce whatever risk does exist to a tolerable level.

A WORD TO THE COOK

The recipes in *Catch of the Day* have been developed in a home kitchen and are meant for home cooks. No fancy equipment is necessary (with the exception of a food processor or a blender); no searching for exotic products that you can't find in a well-supplied supermarket. Mindful of the time expended in cleaning up after a meal, I have tried to minimize the use of numerous pots, pans, bowls, and utensils.

In keeping pace with today's eating style, these recipes are relatively lean. Butter has not been banished from the kitchen, but it is used sparingly. The same goes for cream, eggs, fats, and sodium. There are a few recipes for deep-fried fish, but I have supplied instructions to help minimize absorption of the cooking oil into the finished product. Since most people are aware of the many health benefits derived from a low-fat, low-salt diet, I rely on my readers to use their own judgment in substituting margarine for butter and in using a minimum amount of salt.

I also understand that many people employed outside the home are not able to spend too much time in the kitchen. To that end, although there are a few special-occasion recipes that take longer to make, I have designed the bulk of the recipes for after-work preparation and cooking. Each recipe comes with exact timings for preparation, cooking, chilling, or marinating. Prep time was measured without undue haste, but not without the assumption of some proficiency in the kitchen. My stopwatch started the moment I began to work on the first step of the recipe—after all the required ingredients were on the counter. Getting everything together in advance is a good work habit that I gleaned from experienced chefs—it saves time and frustration, and the results are always better.

I also urge readers to read through a recipe completely *before* attempting to make a dish. Often instructions call for an ingredient that has to be thawed or used at room temperature. Reading a recipe through beforehand can save you time and increase efficiency in the kitchen.

The main purpose of this book is to emphasize that fish is one of the easiest foods to prepare and, if purchased fresh from a reliable source, one of the healthiest and most delicious. The recipes that follow will, I hope, encourage you to make fish a frequent item in your menu planning.

General Information

HOW TO BUY AND STORE FISH

Buy your fish in a top-quality fish store, where the counters are clean, the fish are kept on ice, and the store personnel are cooperative and informed about the origins of the fish and how to cook them properly. A good fish store doesn't smell fishy, either, because really fresh fish don't have a pungent odor, just a clean, briny sea smell.

When you shop for fish, look for the following indicators of freshness:

Whole fish: Eyes are clear and bright, not cloudy (unless they have been in direct contact with ice for a prolonged period). The gills are bright red and moist, not brown or sticky. The stomach cavity is clean and smells fresh, and the flesh is firmly attached to the rib bones and smooth, lustrous, and firm to the touch.

Fillets and fish steaks: Both of these cuts smell fresh and look freshly cut and firm. Their color is pure and translucent, with no discolorations or dried-out areas. Fillets and steaks are not sitting in pools of liquid.

If fish is packaged on plastic foam plates and wrapped in plastic, you may find it more difficult to ascertain freshness. Avoid packages with liquid in them, and run your fingers over the plastic wrapping, especially at the bottom and sides. If your fingers come away smelling fishy, do not buy the product.

It is best to buy fish fresh on the day you plan to use it. Remember, it has already traveled from the ship to the wholesaler to the retailer. During warm-weather months, try to buy fish on your way home or have the store pack it in ice for you.

If you have to keep the fish for a day or so before using, place it, still wrapped, in the coldest part of the refrigerator. If space allows, place the fish in a deep pan, along with a plastic bag of ice. Check periodically to pour off any water that collects in the bottom of the pan and to replace any melted ice.

Take a tip from restaurant chefs and keep fish in the refrigerator until the very last minute before cooking. You will have accurate control of timing the cooking if you always start with cold fish, and it will ensure that the fish is as fresh as possible.

When working with the fish on the counter, use two different areas or two different cutting boards for the raw and the cooked fish. This separation eliminates the danger that bacteria from the uncooked fish may contaminate the cooked fish. Always scrub the area well with soap and hot water after preparing the fish for cooking.

DRESSING AND FILLETING WHOLE FISH

When you buy seafood from a fish store, it can be cut and prepared according to your specifications. However, you'll save money and know that the fish is really fresh if you prepare it yourself for cooking. Dressing a whole fish is not a difficult or time-consuming task since the anatomy of a fish is simple. You will need a few tools for preparing the fish:

A very sharp fish filleting knife with a flexible 9-inch blade

A small sharp knife to cut away rib bones

A medium to large cleaver for cutting through bones

Fish tweezers for pulling out small bones

Kitchen shears or scissors for cutting off fins and gills

A wooden mallet

Most fish must be scaled, a task usually performed at the fish store. But if you are presented with a just-caught fish, you can do it yourself. Spread out lots of newspapers or work in an area that can be thoroughly rinsed. To scale a fish, use a professional fish scaler, the back of a sturdy knife, or a large heavy spoon, and scrape along the body of the fish from the tail to the head, using short, firm strokes. Rinse the fish thoroughly.

Flatfish

Flatfish swim horizontally along the sea bottom, both eyes facing upward. Generally, the top of the fish is darker than the bottom. Flatfish have two thin layers of flesh separated by small bones that fan out of the fish's backbone. Another set of small bones is attached to the upper and lower fins. The flatfish family includes sole, turbot, flounder, haddock, whiting, pollock, cod, cusk, halibut, and sand-dab (also called American plaice).

Preparing a Whole Flatfish

1. To remove the skin, cut off the tail, then lay the top (dark) side up. With a sharp knife, scrape the skin where the tail joins the body to produce a small flap of skin. You can also slip in the tip of the knife to pry a flap of skin away from the flesh. (The white underside of the flatfish is left intact because it is tender and prevents the fish from sticking to the pan when it is cooked.)

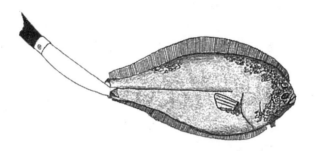

2. Hold the tail end down firmly with one hand. Grasp the loosened flap with the other hand, and pull the skin sharply toward the head. Pull skin off and discard.

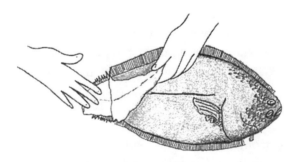

3. Trim off the edge of small bones (the comb) around the fish. Cut the head off on a diagonal close to the gills, cutting more deeply into the belly side to facilitate removing the viscera. Make a small incision

behind the gills and pull out the viscera, which are relatively small in size compared to the body of the fish. Thoroughly clean and wash the cavity.

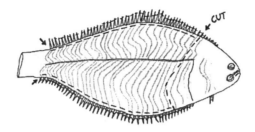

Filleting a Flatfish

1. Remove the skin according to steps 1 and 2 above. With a thin-bladed, sharp, flexible knife, cut down to the backbone along the center of the fish from the head to the tail. Insert the blade at a shallow angle under the central bone in the middle, and, using short strokes, detach the flesh from the bone; then detach the other side of the central fillet. This will release one fillet. Repeat on the other side of the central bone.

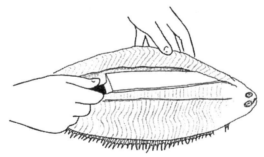

2. Turn the fish over and repeat the filleting on the underside. To skin the two fillets from the underside, lay them skin side down and cut about ½ inch of flesh away from the skin at the tail end. With the fingers of your left hand firmly hold down the exposed piece of skin at the tail end. Insert the knife at a shallow angle beneath the flesh and,

cutting toward the head in short strokes, separate the fillet and skin. Repeat with the other fillet. Trim all four fillets neatly. They are now ready for cooking.

Boning Flatfish for Stuffing

The cavity of flatfish is small in size when its bones are intact. Once the bones are removed, however, the body of the fish becomes flexible and can be spread open to create a cavity for stuffing.

1. Skin the dark, upper side of the fish only. With a sharp, flexible knife cut through the exposed flesh to the backbone, along its entire length. Turn the knife blade toward the outer edge of the fish and, with the knife almost flat against the bones, loosen one fillet to the edge of the fish; do not separate it.

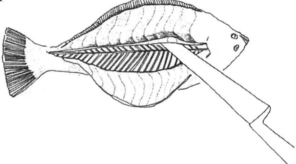

2. Repeat with the other fillet and fold back both loosened fillets, exposing the ribs and backbone. Less flesh is lost if the backbone is removed in sections so, with scissors or kitchen shears, cut through the backbone in several different places.

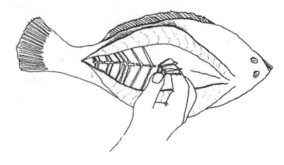

3. Remove and discard all the broken sections of the backbone, which will also have the ribs attached to them. Rinse the fish and pat dry, then stuff.

Roundfish

Roundfish are not truly round but more oval shaped, with the backbone running down the center of the fish between two thick strips of flesh. A line of bones extends upward from the spine; along the bottom of the spine, a double line of bones fans out vertically to enclose the entrails. Roundfish include trout, herring, whitefish, bass, catfish, mackerel, salmon, swordfish, rockfish, monkfish, and red snapper.

Dressing and Filleting Roundfish

1. To gut the fish, if the head has been removed, make a slit along the belly to the vent, the point where the fish curve becomes quite narrow. Pull out the internal organs and scrape any dark blood areas from the backbone. With kitchen shears, cut off the gills and fins.

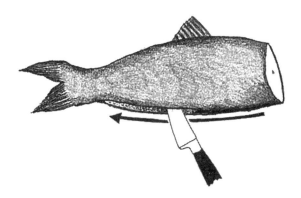

2. Cut through the skin along the backbone without piercing the flesh. Then beginning at the head again, cut close to the backbone with

short strokes, lifting the flesh as you proceed. Continue until the entire fillet has been freed. Turn the fish over and repeat on the other side.

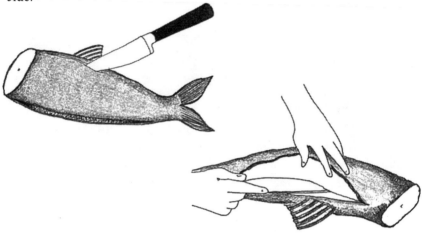

3. To skin the fillets, place them skin side down. With the tail end to the left, slip the knife under the flesh and cut about a half-inch of the flesh away from the skin. Firmly press down on the skin with your left hand. Insert the knife at a shallow angle, and, using short strokes, cut toward the head to completely release the fillet. Trim the two fillets neatly.

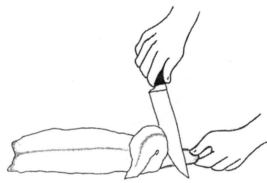

Slicing Roundfish into Steaks

1. Remove the head by first placing the cleaned fish on its belly. Slice into the flesh just behind the gills and firmly push the knife through

the vertebrae and backbone. If the backbone is especially strong, lay a cleaver in the cut and sharply hit it with a wooden mallet or hammer. Lay the fish on its side and cut all the way through the body to separate the head.

2. Put the fish on its belly again, and, using a knife or cleaver, cut through the backbone and body of the fish to make the size steaks you prefer, usually 1 to 1½ inches thick. Turn the fish on its side and slice further through the flesh to detach the steaks.

Boning Roundfish for Stuffing

Roundfish must be boned to increase the size of the cavity for stuffing. The boning technique is different from that used for flatfish, since the ribs and backbone of the roundfish are much thicker.

1. Remove the fins with a knife or scissors. Slit the belly along the entire length of the fish.
2. With one hand lift up one side of the fish. Use a small knife to make little cuts in the membrane that covers the bones, then slide the knife under the rib bones to free them from the flesh. Snap each rib off the backbone with your fingers.

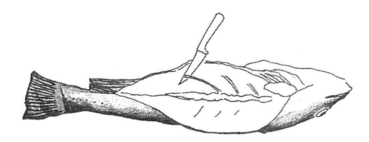

3. To free the backbone, open the fish as wide as possible without tearing the flesh and lightly run the knife down both sides of the backbone. Use kitchen shears to sever the backbone as close to the head as possible. Lift out the backbone and pull it toward the tail, gently nicking the flesh with the knife wherever the bone is still attached. Use the shears again to cut the bone as close to the tail as possible.

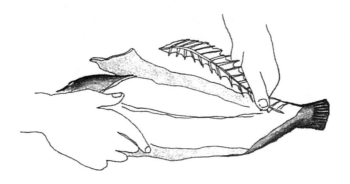

4. Rinse and pat the fish dry, then season the cavity with salt and pepper. Stuff it loosely to prevent the fish from bursting during baking. Push metal skewers through both belly flaps and close the opening by winding string back and forth between the skewers.

How to Prepare Smelts

Smelts are a relatively inexpensive fish and should be utilized more in our kitchens. They have a brisk flavor that can be enjoyed by itself with just a splash of lemon juice, and they can enhance many fish stews and soups. Smelts range from 1½ to 5 inches in length. The smaller varieties are eaten bones and all, since the bones are quite soft. It is best to bone the larger specimens.

In the United States, smelts come onto the market already gutted. Curiously, fresh smelts can be found at supermarket fish counters, but upscale fish shops only carry them frozen. Because smelts are definitely not glamor fish, and are priced accordingly, fancier shops may have less demand for what one French cookbook calls "the pearl of the sea."

Here are the steps to follow for boning larger smelts:

1. Larger smelts usually arrive at the market gutted, with their heads removed. To bone them, enlarge the stomach slit to completely open the fish.

2. With the tip of a small sharp knife, make shallow cuts along either side of the center bone.

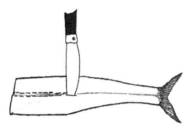

3. Flip up the top end of the bone with the tip of the knife, grasp with your fingers, and pull away the bone. Whether you should remove the tail or not is a matter of preference and esthetics, depending on how you will use the fish. A final tug on the bone will bring the tail off with it. To leave the tail in place, cut across the bone with the tip of the knife.

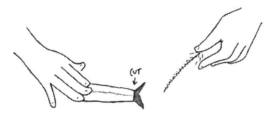

HOW TO BUY AND STORE SHELLFISH AND MOLLUSKS

Shellfish, or crustaceans, are readily identifiable by their inedible hard skins (soft-shell crabs are an exception). Shrimp, crayfish, crab, lobster, even squid, are included in this species.

Shrimp can be purchased fresh in areas close to their natural habitat, but the bulk of the shrimp catch is immediately frozen on board the shrimp boats. Whether fresh or frozen and thawed, shrimp should feel firm to the touch and have a sweet smell. Avoid shrimp with black spots, a limp appearance, or the smell of ammonia, which is a sure sign of deterioration.

Crab can be purchased live or freshly dressed for cooking. Fresh cooked crabmeat is widely available and is sweet smelling and snowy white, not cream colored.

A healthy *lobster* is lively and vigorous, with a curled tail and waving antennas. Lobsters are sold according to size and weight; so-called chicken lobsters, at one pound, are the smallest. Size, however, has nothing to do with taste or quality of the meat.

Squid is a member of the shellfish family; its shell is the thin piece of cartilage inside the mantle. Fresh squid has cream-colored skin with mauve patches. The tentacles should be firm, whole, and intact, and the squid should smell clean and briny, never fishy.

Store live crustaceans in the coldest part of the refrigerator, covered with a moist towel or dampened paper towels. Keep shellfish in the refrigerator until right before cooking to keep them as fresh as possible.

Mollusks include a vast spectrum of shellfish, from univalve periwinkles to popular bivalves such as scallops, oysters, mussels, and clams.

Scallops are rarely sold in their shells in American markets. Very fresh scallops have a clean ivory or cream color without any tinge of gray. Their edges are slightly rounded and smooth. Avoid scallops that are of uniform size with sharply defined edges — they may actually be pieces of fillets of various kinds of fin fish.

The shells of fresh *clams, oysters,* and *mussels* should be tightly closed. If the shells are slightly open and do not snap shut when squeezed or rapped on the counter, discard. Similarly, discard any bivalve that feels very heavy, as it may be dead and the shell filled with sand.

As with other shellfish, place mollusks in the coldest part of the refrigerator and cook within 24 hours of purchase. Clean mollusks just prior to cooking.

CLEANING AND PREPARING MOLLUSKS AND OTHER SEAFOOD

Shrimp

When you prepare shrimp for cooking, peel off the shell from the underside; leave the tail intact for a dressier appearance. Devein the shrimp by making a shallow slit down the back of the shrimp with a paring knife (a bottle opener also works well), and remove the black vein. Deveining is especially important for larger shrimp.

Clams and Oysters

Cultured clams have little or no sand in them, but clams from the sea or bay bottom often do. If you want to make sure, steam a clam open and taste for grit. If you find some, put the clams in salted cold water for about 2 hours to purge themselves, then scrub the shells thoroughly under cold running water with a stiff vegetable brush. If you shuck your own clams, you will need a shucking knife or a sturdy, short-bladed knife to do the job—also use a pair of kitchen gloves to protect your hands. Insert the blade between the shells, moving it gently back and forth. Sever the muscles at the hinge and at the top and bottom of the shells. Do not cut into the clam meat or spill the clam liquor.

Scrub oysters with a stiff vegetable brush to clean them thoroughly. Shucking an oyster is a bit more difficult, so you may prefer the fish store to do it for you. If you do it yourself, you will need basically the same equipment as for clams, and the shucking technique is much the same. Do not use force, or you may break the shell and possibly injure yourself.

Mussels

Although some cookbooks tell you to soak mussels to rid them of their sand, it is not really a good idea. First, mussels don't burrow in the sand but cling to vegetation and solid objects with their strong filaments (byssus) or beard. Second, if mussels come from American mussel farms, they are purged with sea water, thus eliminating any sand or grit they might contain. Most important, mussels are constant feeders and keep their mouths open all the time. To soak them first in any kind of liquid would cause them to give up their sea flavor and take on another character. It's better to risk an occasional grain of sand to keep the briny flavor of the mussel intact.

Although most mussels sold in the United States are precleaned, it is usually necessary to take the following steps in preparing mussels for cooking:

1. Rinse mussels in cold water. Scrub each one with a stiff brush to remove any sand or barnacles on the shell. Grasp the stringy beards between your thumb and a dull knife, and pull them off. If you can't get all of the beard out, remove what you can, and leave the rest, but make sure you cut and scrape away all visible strings.

2. Plunge the scrubbed mussels into a large bowl of cold water, stir them briskly with your hands, then lift them out of the water, leaving any residual sand or grit behind. Rinse one more time under cold running water.

3. Check for any mussels that have not closed in the handling; they are not alive and should be discarded. To be extra sure, pinch the upper and lower shells together. If the mussels close up firmly, they are fine and can be used. If they remain stubbornly wide open, throw them away. If you are suspicious about the health of a mussel, a sure test is to try to move the halves of the shells against one another. The shells of live mussels will not move. If the shell does slide, toss it out. Any mussels that seem exceptionally heavy may indicate that they are full of wet mud and should also be discarded.

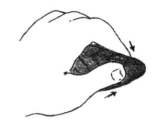

Squid

Technically classified as shellfish, squid are much prized in other parts of the world, particularly in the Orient and around the Mediterranean. Restaurants in the United States often feature squid on their menus but call them by their prettier Italian appellation, *calamari*.

Squid may be one of the greatest untapped sources of protein in the marine world, since 60 to 80 percent of it is edible. Compare that to 20 to 50 percent for vertebrate fish and a mere 20 to 40 percent for shellfish. The fat content of squid varies from 1 to 5 percent, which is considered high for seafood, although that is very low compared to meat.

Although you wouldn't know it by looking at them, squid are very simple to clean. True, some fish stores will do it for you, but it may not always be done as carefully as you would like.

Here are the steps to follow for cleaning squid:

1. Hold the tubelike body (mantle) in one hand and gently twist and pull off the head with the other hand. The intestines should pull right out with the head.

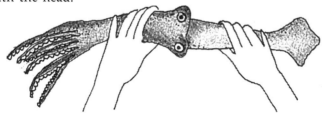

2. Reach inside the body and with your fingers pull out the long, clear pen, or bone, that runs the length of the mantle. Feel for any soft intestinal matter that may have remained inside the body and pull it out with your fingers.
3. Grasp one of the winglike fins and pull downward to remove the mottled skin. Pull off any remaining skin. Reserve the fins.

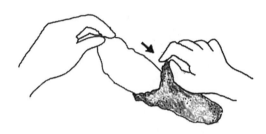

4. Cut the tentacles away from the head at the bony bump just below the eyes. The tentacles and fins can be chopped and used in some recipes although they require long cooking.

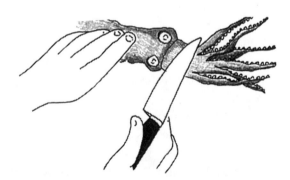

5. Rinse the body well inside and out. It is now ready for cooking and can be stuffed, cut into pieces, or sliced into rings.

Techniques for Cooking Fish

Fish and shellfish are among the easiest of foods to prepare. In fact, if they are fresh and of top quality, the less done to them, the better. But these gifts from the sea also lend themselves to a variety of cooking methods that augment their natural goodness with complementary flavorings and garnishes.

Unlike meat, seafood is naturally tender and requires relatively brief cooking, since the fibrous connective tissue of the fish breaks down rapidly when exposed to heat. On the other hand, too much heat for too long a time quickly damages the fish, causing its flesh to shrink, toughen, and flake apart.

The Canadian Department of Fisheries has developed a simple and reliable method for estimating the proper cooking time for fish: Measure the fish at its thickest point and allow 10 minutes for every inch. This rule of thumb applies to whole fish or thick fish steaks, whatever the cooking method employed.

As reliable as this method is, there are still variables to contend with in the cooking process—variations in oven temperatures and differing heating capacities of materials used in cooking vessels, to name two of the most important. To compensate for these variations, test the fish for doneness. Cut into its thickest part with a knife; if the flesh is opaque and does not cling to the bones, the fish is done. You can also check the internal temperature of a large whole fish with a rapid-response thermometer—it should register 140°F. when the fish is done.

Shellfish need different heats for different species. Still, most need relatively little cooking time, at times nothing more than a quick flash in the pan. The shellfish recipes in this book all give specific directions for timing and testing for doneness.

At one time, the general rule was to cook fish "thoroughly," which usually meant it was overcooked and tasteless. But some chefs and changing food habits have modified attitudes about the degree of doneness we will accept in our fish dishes. The popularity of Japanese sushi and sashimi has also influenced modern fish cookery. Because of the vagaries of shipping and storage conditions, and various health concerns, this book contains no recipes for raw-fish presentations. Cooking times, however, have been modified somewhat to reflect this newer attitude toward enjoyment of seafood at its optimum best.

Professional restaurant chefs also have their convictions relating to the preparation of seafood. The owner of a famous seafood restaurant in Paris, for instance, will not allow a fillet into his kitchen. Most chefs do prefer to cook fish whole, because the bones add succulence to the flesh as they cook together. Some chefs even like to leave the scales on a fish, contending that it helps retain juiciness. And all like to cook fish chilled, when fish has just been removed from the refrigerator. The colder, firmer flesh cooks more slowly, which helps avoid overcooking.

Recipes throughout this book often call for a "nonreactive" pan or skillet. Nonreactive refers to metals that will not react adversely with acid foods, such as tomatoes, citrus, and wines. In these instances, you should use utensils that are made of tin-lined copper, enameled cast-iron, stainless steel with aluminum bottoms, and the newer kitchenware finished with an electrochemical process that makes the surface inert and largely nonstick. Avoid plain aluminum and unlined cast-iron; these materials do react adversely with acidic foods.

A "heat-deflecting pad" refers to any utensil that provides a barrier between the heat source and the bottom of the pan, so that the food cooks more slowly.

SAUTÉING

A simple sauté requires a skillet large enough to hold the fish without crowding, but not so large that the oil or butter burns in the uncovered areas. When sautéing, start with a cold skillet and heat the fat first, whether it is just oil or a combination of oil and butter or margarine. Rinse the fish, pat it dry, and season it with a little salt and pepper. Flour the fish (à la meunière) or not, as you choose. Cook until its underside is golden brown, 3 to 5 minutes for a whole skinned fish. Turn carefully and brown the other side for about the same length of time. Transfer the fish to a platter, garnish with chopped parsley or basil, and serve with lemon.

If a small amount of sauce is desired, pour out the frying oil, add a little fish stock or white wine to the skillet, and simmer briskly. Scrape up the cooking juices and season with salt, pepper, tarragon, or any other herb you fancy. A knob of butter or margarine can be swirled in at the end. Pour over the fish, and serve.

BROILING AND GRILLING

Fish destined for the grill should be coated with a marinade or oil to compensate for the effects of dry-heat cooking. Fatty fish, such as mackerel, bluefish, and tuna, are especially well suited to this technique since they render enough oil to baste themselves and need little extra liquid to prevent parching. For outdoor grilling over a firebed, fish should be contained in a grill basket that permits turning the fish over to cook both sides. Without the basket, one risks losing some of the fish that may stick to the grill. Fish can also be grilled on a ridged cast-iron grill on the stove top, or even in an old-fashioned black cast-iron skillet that is first wiped with oil. Skewered seafood (à la brochette) needs no basket, as long as you use the solid-fleshed varieties, such as scallops, shark, monkfish, tuna, or swordfish.

The intense dry heat of the oven requires that, when broiling fish or shellfish, you use some moisture to protect the fish from drying out. This is usually done by basting with an oil or a liquid—often for lean fish, occasionally for the fattier variety, such as mackerel or tuna. To increase its moisture, the fish can also be treated to a liquid marinade before broiling. Marinades for fatty fish should contain only a small amount of oil, or none at all.

Generally, when broiling any kind of fish, keep the broiling pan at least two inches from the source of heat.

BAKING

Fish can be baked plain in the oven or under wraps, such as bread crumbs or a topping. A whole fish should be basted periodically to prevent the flesh from drying out. Oil, melted butter or margarine (or a combination), stocks, and wines can do the job. Lean fish need more frequent basting. Fillets need a protective bread crumb coating, plus a discreet amount of oil, butter, or margarine and regular basting. Fillets can also be baked as a *gratin*, that is, under a cooked vegetable topping at a temperature of 375°F. Fillets are usually too thin for baking with uncooked gratins; they would be overcooked before the coating was ready.

Another baking method calls for covering the fish to prevent it from drying out. The ultimate dish in this category is pastry-wrapped fish, which is more culinary artistry than necessarily great eating. Or you can simply cover the baking dish to create a moist atmosphere, enclose the fish in aluminum foil or, for a more attractive presentation, in plastic oven bags.

POACHING AND STEAMING

These two moist methods of cooking fish are water related but differ greatly in the temperatures used in each case. When a whole fish or part of a fish is immersed in liquid, as in poaching, never bring it to a boil. If the fish is plunged immediately into hot water, the skin wrinkles and the fish will cook unevenly. Always begin with cool or tepid liquid and slowly bring it to a gentle simmer. The correct cooking temperature of the liquid is between 175° and 180°F. For large whole fish, you will need a rectangular fish poacher. Smaller whole fish can be poached in an oval casserole. Once the water reaches its quiet simmer, cook 10 minutes per inch of thickness. The best poaching liquid is a court bouillon (see page 28), which you can season as you wish.

Steaming means the fish is cooking over the water, not in it. You can use a wok fitted with a rack upon which you place a plate with the fish. (Rub the fish first with oil before steaming to prevent its flesh from sticking to the plate or rack.) Electrical steamers also do a very efficient job. It's not necessary to add flavors to the steaming liquid, since the fish cooks too quickly to allow penetration of the flavors into the flesh. It is much better to put any flavorings directly on, or under, the fish.

There is another steaming method that works just as well and has the added benefit of minimal cleanup afterward: Season the fish fillets or steaks, place them on a large sheet of plastic wrap, and seal tightly. (Or slip the fish and seasonings into a zip-lock plastic bag and close tightly.)

Place package in a steamer, or in a skillet with simmering water. The cooking water does not penetrate to the fish, which then steams in its own juices.

DEEP-FRYING AND STIR-FRYING

Many people do like to deep-fry fish, and although there are only a few recipes that call for deep-frying in this book, the technique is described here. This method reduces the absorption of the oil into the fish, resulting in a crispier, tastier dish.

There is one cardinal rule for deep-frying: an oil temperature of 375°F. This high heat causes the protein in the skin or surface flesh to coagulate and form a seal that protects and preserves the flavor of the fish. This same temperature also cooks batter-coated fish without browning it before the fish within is cooked. It is not necessary to invest in a deep-fryer. An old-fashioned black cast-iron skillet is fine, but any wide, deep skillet will work for small amounts of frying. Use any good-quality polyunsaturated oil.

Chinese stir-frying is hot and quick, using a minimal amount of oil. The food is cut into small pieces and, once in the wok or skillet, kept in almost constant motion to keep the pieces separate and to cook them evenly.

Basic Ingredients and Procedures

The following standard ingredients and procedures are required in a number of recipes throughout this book. Rather than repeat in each recipe, they are placed here for easy reference.

STAPLE INGREDIENTS

Oil

Oil is specified as a cooking medium in many of the recipes. Often olive oil is called for, both for its flavor and its healthful properties. If a less assertive oil is desired, or a type of oil is not specifically given, the choice is up to you. There are many good polyunsaturated oils on the market that are suitable for cooking fish, including canola, safflower, soybean, sunflower, corn, peanut, and sesame oils.

Salt

Although at times certain amounts of salt and pepper are listed in the ingredient list for a particular dish, the quantities are meant only to be guidelines. You may want to add more, or less. When an amount is not specified, or says "to taste," salt and pepper can be added in very sparing amounts, or not at all.

Herbs and Spices

Let your palate be your guide when seasoning these dishes. One way is to add a bit less of the spice or herb that the recipe calls for, cook for a minute or two, then taste and make any necessary adjustments. On the subject of herbs, many cookbooks instruct you to use one-third the amount of dried herbs to fresh. But the strength of dried herbs varies enormously, depending on the initial freshness of the dried product, storage conditions, and how long they have been on your kitchen shelf. Use fresh herbs whenever possible, since there is no substitute for their individual flavoring oils, which impart a subtly assertive taste to a dish.

Butter and Cream

The recipes in this book, with some exceptions, do not call for high-calorie ingredients such as heavy cream. The exceptions are special party dishes or creamed soups, where the addition of a little extra light or heavy cream makes a noticeable difference in taste and texture. But, in each case, the *minimum* amount of cream is specified—an amount that should not be detrimental to a healthy diet. If desired, you may substitute half-and-half for light or heavy cream in many of the recipes. If a recipe lists butter in the ingredients, the health-conscious reader can always substitute margarine.

Fish Stock

If you can boil water, you can make fish stock. Stock consists of nothing more than boiling fish heads and bones together with some flavoring ingredients. You need only 30 minutes of simmering time to produce a full-flavored fish stock. Any longer, actually, will change the flavor for the worse. Unlike meat and poultry, the gelatin in fish bones is readily available and does not need lengthy cooking to leach into the water. In fact, chilled fish stock jells to varying degrees, depending on the ratio of bones to water.

You may find it most efficient to make a sizable quantity of fish stock, pour it into various sized containers, and freeze it. Then if you need just a cupful for a sauce, or a quart for poaching, select an appropriate-size container and defrost. Once you make your own fish stock and see how easy and inexpensive it is (most fish stores will give you the bones for free) you will not return to using bottled clam juice. The bottled juice, fine in an emergency, lacks body and depth of flavor. It's also pretty expensive.

PREPARATION TIME   10 minutes
COOKING   30 minutes

4 pounds bones and heads of lean
  white fish, such as snapper,
  flounder, cod, halibut, haddock,
  or sole
1 large onion, chopped or thinly
  sliced

10 parsley stems*
½ teaspoon salt
2 cups dry white wine
8 cups water
6 peppercorns

1. Rinse the bones and heads thoroughly and remove any gills from the heads. (The gills deteriorate quickly and can affect the taste of the stock.) Also discard skin. Select a nonreactive 6- to 8-quart pot. Add all remaining ingredients, except the peppercorns, and bring to a boil. Reduce heat and simmer gently for 30 minutes, skimming off any

foam that rises. Add the peppercorns for the last 5 minutes of cooking.
2. Strain the fish stock through a cloth-lined sieve, cool, and decant into various containers. Freeze. If the fish stock is kept refrigerated, it should be boiled every 2 days to prevent spoiling.

Makes 1½ to 2 quarts.

*Parsley leaves tend to darken the pale stock, so it's best not to use them.

Court Bouillon

With the exception of plain water, court bouillon is the mildest medium for poaching. It is actually lightly flavored water, but it can be varied to suit the recipe or your whim.

PREPARATION TIME   10 minutes
COOKING   30 minutes

1 large onion, sliced
1 large carrot, sliced
1 large leek, sliced
1 celery rib, sliced
12 parsley stems (without leaves)
A pinch dried thyme

1 bay leaf
6 cups water
Salt
2 cups dry white wine
4 or 5 peppercorns

1. Put all the vegetables, herbs, and water in a large nonreactive pot. Season with a pinch of salt, bring to a boil, reduce the heat, cover, and simmer for about 15 minutes.
2. Pour in the wine and simmer for an additional 15 minutes, adding the peppercorns for the last few minutes. Strain the court bouillon, and refrigerate or freeze.

Makes about 2 quarts.

Chicken Stock

Chicken stock can be refrigerated or frozen. If you intend to freeze it, decant it into several containers for use at different times. If it is refrigerated, bring to the boiling point every two days to prevent spoilage.

PREPARATION TIME   10 minutes
COOKING   2½ hours

4 pounds chicken pieces, including
   leftover bones, necks, gizzards,
   and trimmings (no livers)
4 quarts water
4 carrots, sliced

2 onions, sliced
2 celery ribs
1 tomato
6 parsley sprigs
Salt and pepper

1. Put the chicken in a stockpot, and pour in the water, which should cover the pieces by about 2 inches. Over low heat, bring to a boil, skimming off the scum that rises to the surface. When all the scum has been removed, add the carrots, onions, celery, tomato, and parsley. Add just a little salt, partially cover, and simmer for about 2 hours. Occasionally skim any fats that collect on the surface. Taste for seasonings, and add salt and pepper, if necessary.
2. Strain the stock through a colander into a large bowl, cool, and refrigerate. The next day remove and discard the layer of fat that has congealed on the surface.

Makes about 2 quarts.

Beef Stock

Several recipes in this book call for beef stock in the sauces. Although commercial beef broth can be used, the canned version is high in sodium, and the results are incomparably better using homemade stock.

If you freeze beef stock, decant it into several containers. If it is refrigerated, bring to the boiling point every couple days or so to prevent spoilage.

PREPARATION TIME   15 minutes
COOKING   6 hours

About 2 pounds beef bones, sawed
  into 2-inch pieces
4 carrots, thickly sliced
3 large onions
1 celery rib, broken in half
About 4½ quarts water

About 2 pounds lean beef
2 cloves
1 leek tied up with 10 parsley
  sprigs and 2 bay leaves
4 cloves garlic, unpeeled
Salt and pepper

1. Preheat oven to 450°F. Scatter the beef bones, carrots, 2 of the onions cut into quarters, and the celery in a roasting pan. Roast the bones and vegetables until they become dark brown, about 40 minutes. Turn and baste the browning ingredients several times with the rendered liquids. A lot of smoke is inevitable, but this is an essential step in achieving good color in the finished stock.
2. Transfer the browned bones and vegetables to a large stockpot. Pour off the fat, add 1 cup of water to the roasting pan, and deglaze by scraping up all the juices solidified on the bottom. (Placing the pan over a flame helps the deglazing.) Add these juices to the stockpot along with the beef.
3. Add the remaining water to the stockpot; there should be enough to cover the ingredients by at least 2 inches. Push the cloves into the remaining onion, add to the pot with the leek herb bouquet, garlic, and a little salt. Bring the water to a simmer, and skim off any scum that rises to the surface. Partially cover, and simmer for about 5 hours, occasionally skimming any fats that collect on the surface. The lean beef can be removed after 2 hours and used in salads and other dishes. Add the pepper for the last 15 minutes of cooking. Taste the stock and correct seasoning, if necessary.
4. Strain the stock through a colander into a large bowl, cool, and refrigerate. The next day remove and discard the layer of fat that has congealed on the surface.

Makes about 2 quarts.

Tomato Sauce

When tomatoes are not in season, it is better to use canned whole plum tomatoes.

PREPARATION TIME   15 minutes
COOKING   50 minutes

3 tablespoons olive oil
1 cup chopped onions
1 carrot, peeled and sliced
6 large fresh peeled, seeded, and
    juiced tomatoes, or 4 cups
    drained canned tomatoes

½ teaspoon fresh or dried thyme
½ teaspoon fresh or dried basil
1 teaspoon sugar (optional)
1 teaspoon salt (optional)

1. In a nonreactive 2-quart saucepan, heat the oil and stir in the onions and carrot. Cover and cook for about 5 minutes.
2. Chop tomatoes and add to the pot with the thyme, basil, sugar, and salt. Cook gently, uncovered, until the sauce becomes thick, about 45 minutes. Stir often, scraping the bottom to prevent the sauce from sticking.
3. Pass the sauce through a food mill (do not purée in a food processor or blender). Taste for seasonings and correct, if necessary.

Makes about 4 cups.

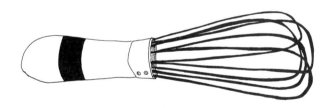

Pesto

The word *pesto* means paste in Italian, since traditionally the ingredients were ground to that consistency in a mortar. Pesto is usually used over hot pasta, or as an addition to thick soups. Its pungent herbal essence can transform the most timid dish into a gustatory experience. Pesto's strength, of course, is variable — Italian cooks (especially in its home port of Genoa) add and subtract ingredients to suit their individual tastes. This recipe is for basic pesto, without nuts or cheese, which can be added if desired.*

Do not buy commercial pesto sold in jars. The manufacturing process "cooks" the sauce, which results in a loss of flavor and authenticity. Pesto can be bought frozen, but it is much better, and cheaper, to prepare it yourself during the summer months when fresh basil is readily available. Put the pesto into small jars, filling them only to about two-thirds full, and freeze.

You can make pesto by hand, but it is far easier and more convenient to use a blender or food processor. Small batches can also be prepared in an electric mini-grinder.

PREPARATION TIME 5 minutes

2 cups fresh basil leaves	½ teaspoon black pepper
2 to 3 tablespoons chopped garlic	Approximately ¾ cup virgin olive
1 teaspoon salt	oil

Put the basil leaves, garlic, salt, and pepper into a food processor or blender. Process in short bursts to chop the leaves and reduce their volume. With the motor running, slowly add the oil in a thin stream.

Makes about 1½ cups.

---

*To transform this basic pesto into a sauce for pasta, add ¼ cup pine nuts or walnuts and ½ cup freshly grated Parmesan or Romano cheese. Do not heat the pesto on the stove. For a better consistency, add a little hot water to the pesto, ideally some of the water in which you have cooked the pasta.

Chive Sauce

This sauce can be made several days in advance, covered tightly, and refrigerated. Bring to room temperature before serving.

PREPARATION TIME   5 minutes
STANDING   1 hour

½ cup low-fat yogurt
¼ cup sour cream
¼ cup buttermilk
Salt and pepper

2 teaspoons rice wine vinegar or
    white wine vinegar
½ cup snipped fresh chives

In a bowl, whisk all ingredients, except the chives. When quite smooth, stir in the chives. Let stand for at least 1 hour before serving.

Makes 1 cup.

METHODS FOR PREPARING VEGETABLES

Some of the vegetables called for in this book are prepared using special culinary techniques. None of these techniques are difficult or time consuming, and all can be accomplished by anyone in a home kitchen. To save space and unnecessary repetition, these methods are described below.

Peeling Tomatoes

Plunge tomatoes into boiling water for a few seconds, remove with a skimmer, cool, and peel. If the recipe specifies "seeded," cut the tomatoes in half, and gently squeeze out the seeds and juice with your hands. The remaining pulp can be sliced or chopped, depending on the recipe.

Peeling and Roasting Red Peppers

To peel red peppers, steam them for about 20 minutes in a covered colander placed over a pot of simmering hot water. Place the steamed peppers in a paper bag, close, and let stand for 10 minutes. The skins will then have softened enough so that they can be peeled off with a small knife. Pull out the stem and remove the seeds and membranes.

If a roasted flavor is desired, place the peppers in a baking dish, and broil, turning them, until all surfaces are blackened. (Tongs are ideal for turning peppers because they can grasp the stems.) Place the charred peppers in a paper bag, close, and put aside for at least 10 minutes to allow the steam time to soften the skins. Then peel.

Making a Chiffonade

A bed of shredded lettuce, called a *chiffonade,* makes an appealing background for fish salads and other cold dishes. The French root of the word is *chiffon,* which does not mean a gauzy fabric but rather rags or scraps. To prepare, wash and dry lettuce leaves. For soft lettuces, such as leaf, Boston, or romaine, stack several leaves at a time and roll them cigarette-fashion. Then cut across into ¼-inch slices, or any desired width. For firm lettuce, such as iceberg, cut the head into quarters, then slice across.

Jalapeño or Other Types of Chili Pepper

To be absolutely safe, wear rubber or plastic gloves when working with hot peppers. Remember, it's the interior of the pepper that is most volatile—the seeds and the white membranes. Cut off the stem end, and, with a small knife, split the pepper in half lengthwise. Carefully cut out the seeds and membrane with the tip of the knife; discard. Always wash your hands and the counter surface you used after handling hot peppers.

Using Tomatillos

There are a number of recipes in this book that call for tomatillos, either as a part of a recipe or as a garnish. Tomatillos are plum-size, greenish yellow fruits that are essential ingredients in many Mexican dishes and salsas. Their lemony-herbal flavor is unique, and, once tried, will be something you'll want to use again and again in salads and main courses.

Tomatillos are usually available in the vegetable sections of supermarkets; if you can't find them in your area, try the following substitute: Blanch the rind of one lemon for 10 minutes, remove, and chop. Add 2 tablespoons chopped fresh parsley and mix. It's not a tomatillo, but the flavor is close enough to make the difference in the recipe.

How to Julienne

The food processor can turn any vegetable into julienne (short, thin sticks) quickly and easily. The pressure of the machine, however, tends to soften the cut vegetables. I much prefer to hand-cut the vegetable into ¼- or ⅛-inch slices, stack several of them, then cut through again into thin sticks. The finished product should be between 1½ and 2 inches long. Practice on a zucchini and see how easy it is. The knife must be sharp.

How to Make Matchsticks

Matchsticks are a smaller version of the julienne. They should be 1½ inches at the most, and as close to ⅛-inch wide as possible.

How to Smash Garlic

Smashed garlic is *not* crushed by means of a garlic press. It is quite simply "smashed," which is a fast way to get much of the inner garlic flavor without chopping it. The more surfaces of the garlic clove that are exposed, the more oils are released. Place the garlic on a sturdy work surface, lay the broad part of a chef's knife over the garlic, and hit it with the side of your clenched fist. A small heavy pot will achieve the same results.

CHAPTER ONE

Hors d'Oeuvres

OYSTER

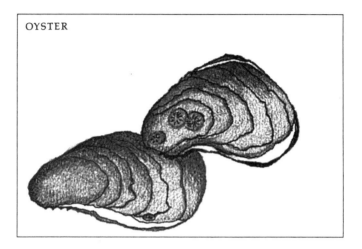

Hors d'oeuvres literally means "outside of the work," indicating that these tasty morsels are meant to whet the appetite for greater things to come. If served before a full dinner, they should be light indeed, and these seafood nibbles admirably do the job. They tempt but never overwhelm.

Tiny Tuna Kebabs

The beauty of these tidbits is that you can prepare them in advance and just flash them under the broiler. They may be small but their flavor is big—piquant, with just a touch of tartness.

PREPARATION TIME   12 minutes
CHILLING   about 30 minutes
MARINATING   at least 1 hour
BROILING   30 seconds to 1 minute

½ pound tuna or marlin steak
  in 1 piece

Marinade

¼ cup light soy sauce
2 teaspoons dark brown sugar
2 teaspoons minced fresh ginger
2 teaspoons ground coriander
2 tablespoons red wine vinegar

2 tablespoons oil
1 tablespoon sherry
1 clove garlic, minced
¼ teaspoon crushed hot red
  pepper flakes

About 28 toothpicks

1. Tightly cover the fish with plastic wrap and place in the freezer to chill and firm the flesh, about 30 to 45 minutes. Unwrap and cut the fish into very thin slices, each about ½-inch wide and 1 by 2 inches long. Sizes are approximate and will depend on the shape of the particular tuna steak.
2. While the tuna is chilling, mix all marinade ingredients in a medium-size bowl. Add the sliced tuna to the marinade, turn with your hands to coat all the fish thoroughly, cover, and refrigerate for at least 1 hour. The fish can marinate as long as 6 hours in the refrigerator.
3. Soak the wooden toothpicks in a bowl of warm water for at least 30 minutes. (This will prevent them from catching fire under the broiler.) Lift the fish slices from the marinade and thread each piece onto a toothpick—that is, shove the toothpick down into the piece of

fish then up through the fish again. Place the kebabs on a baking sheet. If prepared in advance, refrigerate before cooking.

4. Preheat the broiler and broil the kebabs for about 30 seconds to 1 minute or just until the flesh firms and sizzles. Serve at once.

Makes about 28 kebabs.

HINT Bitter oils can lurk in the green sprout growing in the center of fresh garlic, the only part of the clove that is still growing. If necessary, cut the garlic in half and pry out the green sprout with the tip of the knife and discard.

Rosy Fish Spread

You can use almost any fish in this recipe except the oily or firm-textured variety such as swordfish or monkfish. You can also use leftover cooked fish. This savory spread can be made a day or two in advance and refrigerated—its flavors will blend even better.

PREPARATION TIME   8 minutes

STEAMING   3 to 10 minutes

CHILLING   at least 1 hour

½ pound fish fillets, such as cod, flounder, sole, salmon, or bass
1 tablespoon capers, rinsed, drained, and chopped
¼ cup part skim milk ricotta
2 tablespoons sour cream
1 to 1½ tablespoons ketchup
½ teaspoon Worcestershire sauce

Few drops hot red pepper sauce
Salt and pepper
2 tablespoons chopped fresh parsley
About thirty-six 1-inch melba toast rounds
2 tablespoons capers, or chopped fresh parsley (optional)

1. Envelop the fish in plastic wrap and cook according to the directions for poaching or steaming on page 24. Timing will depend on the thickness of the fillet, anywhere from 3 to 10 minutes.
2. Place the cooked fish in a mixing bowl and mash with the back of a fork. Add the capers and mix them in.
3. In a separate small bowl, stir together the ricotta, sour cream, ketchup, Worcestershire sauce, hot pepper sauce, and salt and pepper. Pour this sauce over the fish and mix well. Gently fold in the parsley. Cover the spread and refrigerate for at least 1 hour.
4. Scoop about ½ tablespoon of the rose-colored spread onto a toast round and spread over the surface. Place a caper or pinch of parsley in the center, if desired.

Makes about thirty-six 1-inch canapés.

Fish Mousse Canapés

The zip in this mousse comes from the horseradish. You can decide, by adjusting the amount of horseradish, just how zippy you like it. Although zucchini rounds are suggested as the base, toast rounds can also be used. A larger version of this hors d'oeuvre can be made by spreading the mousse on a slice of toast, then cutting the toast into quarters, either in triangles or long strips. You can use leftover fish in this recipe, if you wish, and these canapés can be prepared, placed on a baking sheet, and refrigerated until needed.

PREPARATION TIME   15 minutes
COOKING AND COOLING   about 20 minutes
BROILING TIME   2 to 3 minutes

¼ pound fish fillets, such as flounder, pollock, sole, halibut, or cod; or leftover cooked fish
1 cup Fish Stock (see page 27) or clam broth
½ cup part skim milk ricotta
2 tablespoons coarsely chopped fresh cilantro, or 1 tablespoon chopped fresh mint

3 tablespoons frozen orange juice concentrate
A few drops hot red pepper sauce
Salt and pepper
1½ to 2 teaspoons prepared horse-radish
¼ pound zucchini
About 3 tablespoons bread crumbs
1 fresh tomato (optional)

1. Poach the fish according to the directions for Summer Fish Salad (page 195), using Fish Stock instead of milk. Cool, then flake into pieces.
2. If the ricotta is watery, drain off the liquid; some brands contain more whey than others. Put the ricotta into a food processor or blender* and add the fish, cilantro or mint, orange juice concentrate, hot red pepper sauce, salt and pepper, and 1 teaspoon of the horseradish. Pulse a few times; then purée the mixture. Taste and add ½ teaspoon more of the horseradish, if desired. There will be about 1 cup mousse.
3. Cut the zucchini into ¼-inch rounds. Cover each one with about ½ tablespoon of the mousse, sprinkle with about ¼ teaspoon bread crumbs, and place on a baking sheet.

4. If you use the tomato, cut off a slice from the top, then cut vertically to remove the skin and a thin layer of flesh beneath it. Cut the tomato into little strips and use to decorate the canapés. One small piece can be placed in the center, or make a small **V** with 2 pieces.
5. Broil the canapés for about 2 minutes, or until the tops are lightly browned.

Makes about thirty-two 1-inch canapés.

*To prepare the mousse in a blender, first put the Fish Stock and orange juice concentrate into the container. Add the ricotta and all seasonings and purée. Flake the fish into smaller pieces than for a food processor and add it to the mixture, ½ cup at a time. If the blender seems to strain, add a few tablespoons more Fish Stock.

Tangy Oriental Shrimp

Although these shrimp would be just as delicious served piled up in a bowl, it pays to give them an extra glamorous treatment. This is as simple as providing a nice color contrast — the pink shrimp against green lettuce. Tangy Oriental Shrimp would also make a satisfying first course or sparkling salad.

The shrimp taste best if allowed to marinate for at least 24 hours.

PREPARATION TIME   10 minutes
COOKING   about 10 minutes
MARINATING   24 hours

1 pound medium shrimp	2 teaspoons light soy sauce
1 cup tomato juice	¼ teaspoon hot red pepper
1 cup unsweetened grapefruit	sauce
juice (canned, frozen, or fresh)	Freshly ground pepper to taste
5 thin slices fresh ginger	4 to 5 soft lettuce leaves
2 cloves garlic, smashed (see page	1 tablespoon sesame seeds
36)	

1. Rinse the shrimp and put them in a deep 6- to 8-cup nonreactive pot. Add all remaining ingredients except lettuce and sesame seeds.
2. Place the pot over medium heat and very slowly bring to a simmer. It should take 7 to 10 minutes to reach the simmering point. Stir several times to rotate the shrimp on the top and bottom. Watch the shrimp carefully, they should be cooked in about 30 seconds, 1 minute at the most. The shrimp are cooked when they become rather firm and white. With a skimmer, remove the shrimp and place in a bowl. Allow the cooking liquid to cool, then pour over the shrimp. Cover and refrigerate for at least 24 hours.
3. Peel the shrimp. Leave the tail intact: it adds a nice decorative note. Tear the lettuce into 1- to 1½-inch pieces. Place 1 shrimp on each lettuce bit, dip your finger into the sesame seeds and touch the top of each shrimp. A scattering of the seeds will adhere to the shrimp and give them a flavorful finishing touch.

Serves 12 to 15.

HINT   Although it's often recommended to freeze fresh ginger to extend its usefulness, ginger turns mushy once defrosted and then cannot be grated or minced. Just cover the fresh ginger closely with plastic wrap and keep in the vegetable drawer of the refrigerator; it will stay fresh for months.

Ecrevisses au Pernod

(SHRIMP WITH PERNOD)

The licorice-flavored alcohol in this shrimp broth adds a bitingly refreshing note. This is a convivial party dish when the shrimp are served in the shell; have plenty of paper napkins on hand. Obviously, a more refined presentation calls for peeling them before serving. In either case, allow the shrimp to marinate intact in their shells.

PREPARATION TIME   2 minutes, plus 10 minutes for peeling
COOKING   12 minutes
MARINATING   24 hours

1½ cups water
½ onion, coarsely chopped
1 bay leaf
½ tablespoon rosemary, preferably fresh
½ teaspoon hot red pepper sauce

2 tablespoons crushed peppercorns
½ lemon
¼ to ⅓ cup licorice-flavored liqueur (Pernod, ouzo, or arak)
1 pound medium shrimp

1. Pour the water into a 2-quart pot, add the onion, bay leaf, rosemary, pepper sauce, and peppercorns. Squeeze in the juice of the lemon and toss in the peel or rind of the lemon as well. Bring the water to a boil, cover, and simmer for 10 minutes.
2. Add the liqueur and shrimp, cover, and simmer gently for about 2 minutes, or until the shrimp just begin to turn a bright pink. Remove from the heat immediately. (It is important not to cook the shrimp completely at this point since they continue to cook in the hot broth.) Still covered, put the pot aside to cool to room temperature, then refrigerate for at least 1 day.
3. For a simple presentation, drain the shrimp and heap them into a bowl. For a more showy dish, peel each shrimp, push a toothpick through its thick end, and plunge the other end of the toothpick into a grapefruit. The finished centerpiece will resemble a porcupine. Guests can then pull out the toothpicks and enjoy their tasty morsels.

Serves 12 to 15.

HINT   Peppercorns have a better flavor when they are ground in a mortar and pestle or placed on a sturdy work surface and smashed with the bottom of a heavy pot or with a mallet.

Stuffed Mussels

Mussels make obliging cocktail tidbits since they provide their own little dishes. Furthermore, they are inexpensive, enticingly plump and meaty, and easy to prepare.

You can make the stuffing the day before, refrigerate it, and then bring it back to room temperature before using.

PREPARATION TIME   25 minutes
COOKING   (if steamed) 1 to 2 minutes
BROILING   2 to 3 minutes

Stuffing

⅓ cup polyunsaturated margarine, softened
¾ cup very fine bread crumbs
2 tablespoons very finely chopped shallots
⅛ teaspoon dried thyme

2 tablespoons lemon juice
3 tablespoons finely chopped fresh parsley
2 tablespoons brandy, dry vermouth, or dry white wine
Salt and pepper

36 mussels (2½ pounds), scrubbed and cleaned (page 17)

1. Cream the margarine in a small deep bowl while slowly adding the bread crumbs. Add remaining stuffing ingredients, then put aside.
2. Open the mussels with a blunt knife. If you prefer, you can first steam them briefly to make them easier to open. (Some juiciness is sacrificed, however.) Discard one of the shells on each mussel and put the other with the mussel in a shallow ovenproof dish.
3. With a broad knife, spread a bit of the stuffing onto each mussel. Preheat broiler and slip the dish under the flame for 2 or 3 minutes, just until the stuffing bubbles and is lightly browned.
4. Place the mussels on a warm platter. Small oyster forks can be provided or even toothpicks. It is also a simple matter for guests to slip the mussel off its shell and eat it using no implements at all.

Serves 12.

Spicy Oysters

People who don't eat raw oysters may approach these tasty morsels with apprehension. The oysters may look raw, but you can assure your guests they have been well cooked. Also, because of the wine and lemon juice used in the marinade, they will keep for a day in the refrigerator.

PREPARATION TIME   4 minutes
COOKING   about 5 minutes
MARINATING   3 hours

1 pint shucked oysters, smallest size available
1 cup dry white wine
Juice of 2 lemons
½ teaspoon vinegar, preferably balsamic or red wine
¼ cup olive oil
2 bay leaves

¼ teaspoon hot red pepper sauce
1 teaspoon freshly ground black pepper
Chopped fresh parsley
Buttered bread squares
Lettuce leaves and tomato wedges (optional)

1. Put the oysters and their liquor in a 4-cup nonreactive pot. Pour in the wine, lemon juice, vinegar, and oil. Add the bay leaves, hot pepper sauce, and pepper. Stir to blend the marinade.
2. Put the pot on medium heat and bring the marinade to the boiling point. As soon as the liquid begins to boil, remove the pot from the heat. Cover and let marinate for at least 1 hour. Refrigerate at least 2 hours to chill.
3. Lift the oysters out of the marinade and place on paper towels. If they are large, cut them in half. Transfer them to a deep serving bowl, spoon on a little of the marinade, and sprinkle with the chopped parsley. Surround the bowl with small squares of buttered bread, preferably rye or whole wheat. The oysters can also be presented on a platter: place each oyster on a small piece of lettuce or bread (or a combination of the two) and arrange in concentric circles. Fan out tomato wedges in a circle in the center.

Serves 12.

HINT   Lemons give up more juice if used when they are at room temperature. If stored in the refrigerator, remove them at least 1 hour before squeezing. Also, to extract more juice, roll the lemon on the counter while pressing on it. This breaks down some of the membranes surrounding the juice sacs.

Grilled Oysters

This is a dish created especially for oyster lovers. The success of this quick recipe depends on the dryness of the skillet and the rapid grilling of the plump mollusks. Since the oysters will exude some juice, it is best not to cook too many at a time—six at the most in one skillet. If you're a super-fast cook you can easily handle two skillets.

Purists usually like their oysters served with just a squeeze of lemon. The salsa, though, provides a snappy edge.

PREPARATION TIME   3 minutes

GRILLING   3 minutes

TO PREPARE OPTIONAL SALSA 1 HOUR IN ADVANCE   5 minutes

Salsa

2 tomatillos (page 35)

1 medium tomato, peeled and seeded, or 2 canned plum tomatoes with ½ fresh tomato for crunchy texture

2 scallions, coarsely chopped

½ jalapeño pepper, coarsely chopped (page 35) (optional)

Salt and pepper

1 tablespoon extra-virgin olive oil (optional)

½ pint shucked oysters, standard size

2 teaspoons oil

Freshly ground black pepper

½ lemon

1. Prepare the salsa at least 1 hour ahead. Husk the tomatillos, cut into quarters, and put in a food processor or a blender. Coarsely chop the tomato and add to the processor or blender with the scallions and jalapeño, if using. Pulse for about 10 seconds to chop the vegetables into small pieces. Do not purée. Scrape into a bowl and season with salt and pepper. If the salsa seems a little dry, stir in the olive oil.
2. Drain the oysters, retaining the liquor, and if they are very large, cut in half. Dry the oysters between several layers of paper towels.
3. Select a heavy skillet, preferably cast iron, wipe it with a teaspoon of oil, and heat until very hot. Slip in the oysters one by one and grill for about 20 seconds; turn over and grill the other side for 10 to 20

seconds more, or just until the second side is also browned a little. Carefully wipe out the skillet to dry, sweep with the oil, and continue grilling the remaining oysters.

4. Place the grilled oysters on a warm platter and season with fresh pepper and lemon juice. Spear with toothpicks and serve while hot. Serve the salsa in a bowl with a small spoon.

Serves 4.

HINT   Save the oyster liquor by putting it in a plastic container and freezing. Use it later in fish soups and stews in place of water or bottled clam juice.

Quick-Smoked Trout Canapés

The smoking technique used here does not require any elaborate equipment. Anyone with a wok or a deep, heavy cast-iron skillet can do it. Two different smoking mixtures are described—one for a delicate smokey flavor, the other for a more emphatic taste. Other fish can be used, even fillets, but only if the skin is attached to one side. The resulting flavor is superb.

PREPARATION TIME 5 minutes
SMOKING 20 minutes

1 pound whole sea trout
  with skin, gutted and head
  removed
2 tablespoons black tea
  leaves
1 tablespoon brown sugar

1 tablespoon juniper berries,
  crushed
Oil
6 slices thinly sliced white bread
  or 24 crackers
1 lime

1. Line the wok or skillet with aluminum foil, allowing at least 3 inches of overhang. Measure onto the foil the tea, brown sugar, and juniper berries, and mix with your fingertips.
2. Place a rack at least 1 inch above the smoking mixture. You can use a small wire stand or cake stand. A stand can also be fashioned out of an ordinary 8-inch disposable foil pie pan: Set it upside down in the pan; if too large, cut a wedge out and pull the ends together to fit. Punch about 10 holes in the pie pan.
3. Oil the fish and place on the smoking rack; if a fillet, place it skin side down. Cover the skillet or wok with another piece of heavy-duty aluminum foil and crimp the edges together with the foil in the bottom of the pan. This will create a tight seal. Cover with a lid. Place the wok or skillet over high heat, and once you can begin to smell the smoking mixture, reduce heat to medium high and smoke the fish for 15 minutes. Turn off heat and let stand for 5 minutes. If smoking fillets, allow only 10 minutes for the smoking, plus 5 minutes for standing.
4. While the fish is smoking, remove the crusts from the bread, toast, and cut each slice diagonally twice, creating 24 triangles.

5. Transfer the trout to a dish and remove the skin and bones. Some of the skin may have stuck to the smoking rack, but that's just less for you to remove.
6. Make a small pile of the smoked fish on a toast triangle or cracker and squeeze a few drops of lime juice over the fish and serve.

Makes about 2 dozen canapés.

VARIATION   For a stronger smoke flavor, use ¼ cup black tea leaves, 2 tablespoons brown sugar, and 1 crumbled bay leaf. For the canapés, 4 slices thinly sliced white bread, ¾ cup low-fat ricotta, and 1 lime. Follow the directions for smoking the trout using this stronger flavored mixture. Smear about ½ tablespoon of ricotta on each toast triangle, top with the smoked fish, and add a few drops of lime juice.

HINT   Although home-smoked fish keeps for several days, it is not thoroughly cured and contains no salt. Therefore, it cannot be kept for as long a period as commercially smoked fish.

First Courses

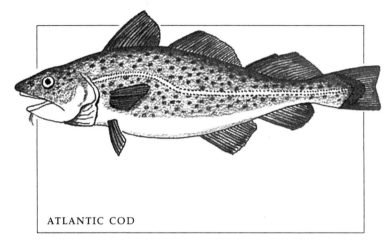

ATLANTIC COD

Serving the right first course can turn any meal into
an occasion. The following recipes have been
designed to please the palate and leave your guests
eagerly anticipating what comes next.

Many of these dishes would also make an excellent
main course for a festive lunch. Gingered Shrimp on
Leeks, for example, is superb served with blanched
snow peas mixed with shredded jicama. Or you could
tuck steamed broccoli or a few potato chips next to
Mediterranean Marinated Fish for a satisfying light
repast. Seafood Terrine is especially appropriate for
this role since it is a light, attractive, and somewhat
sophisticated fare that needs nothing more than a
vegetable dish or a mixed salad to complete the meal.

Grilled Scallops

The cooking procedure for this dish involves nothing more than a quick searing of plump sea scallops. The trick is to sear them so quickly that none of the juices escape. The amount to serve depends on the rest of the menu.

PREPARATION TIME   2 minutes
COOKING   2 minutes

¾ to 1 pound large sea scallops   1 lemon, quartered
½ to 1 teaspoon oil   8 parsley sprigs
Salt and pepper

1. Rinse the scallops and dry on paper towels. Meanwhile heat a heavy 10-inch skillet, preferably cast iron, until very hot. Pour in ½ teaspoon oil, and wipe it over the surface of the skillet with a paper towel.
2. When the oil is almost smoking, place in the skillet as many scallops as will fit without crowding. If necessary, cook them in 2 batches, re-oiling the pan in between. Sear the scallops for about 30 seconds, just until they begin to brown around the edges, then turn. Sprinkle with salt and pepper while the second side sears, an additional 30 seconds or so. Repeat the procedure with the remaining scallops.
3. Place the scallops on warm salad plates, and garnish each one with a lemon wedge and 2 parsley sprigs. Serve at once.

Serves 4.

HINT   Some scallops still have the connective tissue attached. It is identifiable by its color—opaque white, against the pearly translucence of the scallop muscle. Be sure to cut it off before cooking the scallops, as it toughens and interferes with their delicate texture.

Scallops with Parmesan

This simple but elegant shellfish presentation calls for scallops that are absolutely fresh. Frozen scallops will exude too much liquid and ruin the finesse of the dish. The Parmesan also must be fresh, not sprinkled from a box or jar.

PREPARATION TIME 5 minutes
BROILING 2 minutes

12 ounces bay scallops
¼ cup dry white wine
2 teaspoons extra-virgin olive
   oil

A sprinkling of freshly ground
   pepper
2 tablespoons grated Parmesan
   cheese

1. Preheat broiler. Rinse the scallops and pat dry on paper towels. Mix them in a bowl with the wine, olive oil, and pepper. Add three-fourths of the cheese and gently mix together.
2. Divide the scallop mixture among 4 individual gratin dishes or scallop shells. Sprinkle the remaining cheese over the top.
3. Place the dishes on a firm baking sheet and broil for about 2 minutes, or until the tops are lightly browned. Serve at once.

Serves 4.

Mussel Cocktail

Mussels are inexpensive and make an unexpected and interesting presentation. Furthermore, you know you are working with a very fresh product, since mussels cannot be frozen.

You can steam the mussels a day in advance, remove them from their shells, and refrigerate in the cooking broth. When ready to proceed with the recipe, drain off the broth. Cold mussels absorb marinade flavorings more slowly, so allow refrigerated mussels to stand at least two hours in the marinade.

PREPARATION TIME   20 minutes
COOKING   5 minutes
MARINATING   1 hour

3 pounds mussels, scrubbed,
   cleaned, and steamed (page 17)
¼ cup olive oil
¼ cup dry vermouth
Juice of ½ lemon

¼ teaspoon celery seeds
Salt and pepper
¾ cup mayonnaise
¼ cup chopped fresh parsley
Lettuce

1. While the mussels are steaming, prepare the marinade. In a mixing bowl, whisk together the olive oil, vermouth, lemon juice, celery seeds, and salt and pepper.
2. As soon as the mussels are cool enough to handle, remove the shells and drop the mussels into the marinade. Toss gently. Cover and let stand at room temperature for at least 1 hour, stirring occasionally.
3. At serving time, drain the mussels, reserving the marinade. Spoon the mayonnaise into a bowl and beat into it enough of the marinade to make a thin sauce. Fold the mussels into the sauce and stir in the chopped parsley.
4. Heap the mussels into individual lettuce-lined bowls.

Serves 6 to 8.

Gingered Shrimp on Leeks

This is a particularly appealing presentation of golden-tinged pink shrimp served on a mostly white bed. The spicy ginger flavor contrasts nicely with the mellow leeks. A good menu follow-up would be cold poached chicken breasts with herb mayonnaise and a vegetable purée, such as carrots or peas, or both.

The basic leek sauce (without the tomatoes) can be made in advance and refrigerated; just be sure not to reduce the liquid too much, for better reheating later.

PREPARATION TIME   12 minutes
COOKING   15 minutes

2 tablespoons oil
5 slices fresh ginger
½ pound leeks
⅓ cup light cream or half-and-half
½ cup milk
½ cup dry white wine

½ teaspoon ground coriander
Salt and pepper
1 medium tomato, peeled, seeded, and chopped (about 1 cup)
¾ pound medium shrimp, peeled and deveined

1. Pour the oil into a heavy 10- or 12-inch skillet and add the ginger slices. Slowly heat the oil and brown the ginger, pressing the pieces a few times to release the oils. Turn now and then to thoroughly brown both sides. When the slices are a dark brown, cover the skillet and put aside.

2. Clean the leeks (page 201). Cut the leeks into ¼-inch slices and place in a 10- to 12-inch nonreactive skillet. Pour in the cream, milk, and wine, and season with the coriander and a sprinkling of salt and pepper. Cover and cook for about 10 minutes, or until most of the liquid has disappeared. Stir occasionally. If you see some curds around the edges of the pan, ignore them. (The mixture will have a uniform appearance when completely cooked.) There should be enough liquid to make a creamy sauce; if there is too much liquid, remove cover and boil rapidly to evaporate some of the excess moisture. Cover and keep warm.

3. Heat the ginger-flavored oil and discard the ginger slices. Add the shrimp and cook over brisk heat, turning them over and over to quickly cook them, with a browned edge here and there. This should not take more than 1 or 2 minutes. If necessary, stir-fry the shrimp in two batches to avoid overcrowding.
4. Reheat the leeks and stir in the chopped tomato. Make a bed of the creamy leeks on 4 salad plates and top with the gingered shrimp. Serve at once.

Serves 4.

HINT   The ginger-flavored oil can be poured into a jar and refrigerated. Use in sauces and gravies.

Shrimp in Creamy Aspic

This dish makes an attractive beginning to a meal. The pieces of pink shrimp are caught in a delicately flavored mayonnaise aspic, the bright green peas adding additional visual appeal. If you substitute clam juice for the Fish Stock, dilute it by using three-fourths cup juice and one-fourth cup water.

This dish can be prepared a day or two in advance and kept in the refrigerator.

PREPARATION TIME   20 minutes, plus 1 hour for chilling cooked ingredients
COOKING   12 minutes
CHILLING   at least 3 hours

2 cups water
1/4 teaspoon celery seeds
4 slices fresh ginger
1 clove garlic, smashed (page 36)
1/4 teaspoon pepper
1/2 lemon
1/2 pound medium shrimp, unpeeled
1 anchovy fillet
2 tablespoons dry vermouth or white wine
1 cup Fish Stock (page 27)

1 1/2 tablespoons unflavored gelatin
1 cup mayonnaise
1/2 cup low-fat yogurt
2 teaspoons Pesto (page 32)
1 teaspoon rice wine or white wine vinegar
A few drops hot red pepper sauce
Salt and pepper
1/2 cup peas, cooked and chilled
Oil
6 lettuce leaves

1. In a 4-cup pot, boil the water, celery seeds, ginger, garlic, and pepper. Squeeze the lemon juice into the water, then toss in the peel or rind. Cover and cook for 10 minutes.
2. Add the shrimp, stir, and cook just a minute or so, until the flesh firms and turns white. Drain at once. Cool and peel. Cover 3 of the shrimp with plastic wrap and refrigerate. Cut the rest into pieces about 1/4 inch thick. Chill.
3. In a small 1-cup pot, combine the anchovy fillet and vermouth and stir. Simmer slowly over medium heat until the anchovy dissolves into the wine. Cool.

4. Put the Fish Stock in a small pot and sprinkle the gelatin into it. Let stand for about 3 minutes, until the gelatin softens and turns translucent. Put on low heat and, while stirring, bring just to the simmering point. Remove at once from the heat and cool. (The hot liquid will cool faster if transferred to a small bowl.)
5. In a 2-quart bowl, mix the mayonnaise, yogurt, Pesto, vinegar, and hot pepper sauce. Stir in the anchovy-flavored wine, removing any pieces of the fish that have not dissolved. Stir in the cool Fish Stock. Taste and correct seasonings if necessary. Chill until the aspic begins to set but is still soft, 15 to 30 minutes.
6. Meanwhile, lightly oil six 1-cup custard cups or similar molds. Gently stir the shrimp and the peas into the mayonnaise aspic. Spoon the aspic mixture into the cups, tapping the molds on the counter to settle the filling well into the cups. Cover and refrigerate for at least 3 hours.
7. Place a lettuce leaf on a salad plate. With a thin knife dipped in hot water, cut around the molded aspic. Dip the bottom of the mold into hot water and turn the aspic out onto the lettuce. If the aspic proves a little stubborn, slip the knife down to the bottom and give a little tug. Slice the reserved 3 shrimp in half horizontally producing 6 crescent-shaped halves. Place the shrimp garnish on each aspic mold.

Serves 6.

HINT   Gelatin granules should always be softened in a cold liquid before they are dissolved in the hot liquid to be jelled. To do this, pour 2½ teaspoons (one package) over a minimum of ¼ cup liquid and let stand for 5 minutes to soften. The granules will turn translucent at this stage. When completely dissolved in hot liquid, the gelatin will turn clear. Two and a half teaspoons will jell 2 cups of liquid.

Cauliflower with Shrimp Sauce

A little bit of shrimp goes a long way in this unusual appetizer, but their briny flavor dominates the rosy sauce. For the prettiest presentation, the cauliflower should be kept whole, which means cooking it thoroughly so that it can be easily served at the table.

The sauce can be prepared a day in advance, without the shrimp, and then refrigerated. The cauliflower can be cooked several hours ahead of time and kept tightly covered at room temperature, then briefly reheated in a steamer or microwave oven.

PREPARATION TIME   5 minutes
COOKING   25 minutes

½ teaspoon salt
1 medium head cauliflower
1½ tablespoons butter or
   margarine
1½ tablespoons flour
1 cup milk
¼ cup light cream
½ teaspoon anchovy paste

½ teaspoon dry sherry
2 teaspoons lemon juice
¼ teaspoon pepper
A few drops hot red pepper sauce
A good pinch freshly grated nutmeg
6 ounces cooked, peeled, and
   deveined shrimp
Paprika

1. In a large saucepan, bring a large quantity of water to a boil, and add the salt. Meanwhile, wash the whole cauliflower, cutting away all the green leaves, add it to the pan, and cook until tender, about 7 minutes after the water has returned to the boil. Drain well, then cover to keep warm.
2. Meanwhile, melt the butter in a heavy saucepot, stir in the flour, and cook for 2 minutes. Slowly pour in the milk and the cream while stirring with a wire whisk. Add the remaining ingredients except the shrimp and paprika. Taste for seasoning, and correct if necessary. Simmer the sauce for 5 minutes.
3. Cut the shrimp into pieces about ¼-inch thick, reserving 2 whole ones for garnish. Add the pieces to the sauce just before serving.

4. Place the cauliflower head in a deep serving bowl. Spoon some of the hot shrimp sauce over the top, lightly sprinkle with paprika, and garnish with the reserved shrimp. Pour the rest of the sauce into a sauceboat, and pass separately. Provide 2 large spoons for serving the cauliflower.

Serves 4.

Baked Oysters

No special culinary skills are needed for these oysters—a quick scrub and they are ready. Once in the oven the oysters plump up into moist, succulent morsels. As easy as this recipe is, timing is crucial. If the oysters are over-baked, they dry out.

The oysters can be scrubbed a few hours before baking, put in the salt on the baking pan, and refrigerated. If they are cold when first put into the oven, add a few minutes to the baking time.

PREPARATION TIME   10 minutes
BAKING   10 to 15 minutes

4 cups rock salt or Kosher salt	1 teaspoon dry white wine
16 oysters in the shells	2 teaspoons lemon juice
4 tablespoons butter or margarine	Salt and pepper

1. Preheat oven to 450°F. Pour the rock or Kosher salt into a jelly roll pan or other baking pan with sides. Smooth the salt into an even layer.
2. Scrub the oysters under cold running water and arrange them flat side up on the salt, firmly imbedding them in the salt. Place the baking pan in the heated oven for 10 to 15 minutes, or until the oyster shells begin to pop open. Since the oyster muscle has been relaxed by the heat, it is comparatively easy to pry open any oysters that have not yet done so. (Because of differing shell configurations, oysters do not all open at the same time.)
3. While the oysters are baking, prepare the sauce. In a small pot, melt the butter or margarine with the wine, lemon juice, and salt and pepper. Bring the sauce just to a boil and remove at once from the heat. Pour it into 4 individual custard cups.
4. Bring the baking pan with the oysters to the table. Guests serve themselves, 1 oyster at a time. The top shell of the oyster is pulled off, the oyster speared with a fork and dipped into the hot butter sauce.

Serves 4.

HINT   The heavy rock (or Kosher) salt prevents the oysters from tipping over and losing their liquor. Also, because the salt warms up in the oven, it retains heat and keeps the oysters warm at the table.

Herbed Scalloped Oysters

This less rich version of the traditional scalloped oysters makes a lighter beginning to a meal. The addition of a few vegetables and herbs also brings a fresh flavor to the dish. An appealing accompaniment would be a salad of snow peas or green beans tossed with a mild vinaigrette, served at room temperature.

PREPARATION TIME   10 minutes

COOKING   30 minutes

1 pint shucked oysters
2 tablespoons butter or margarine
2 celery ribs, sliced
4 scallions, sliced
40 low-salt saltine crackers (about 4 ounces)
1 teaspoon paprika

1 teaspoon dried thyme
½ teaspoon freshly ground black pepper
1 teaspoon oil
½ cup light cream or half-and-half
A few drops hot red pepper sauce

1. Preheat oven to 425°F. Transfer the oysters to a colander set over a deep bowl and let drain. Melt the butter in a small saucepan, add the celery and scallions, cover, and simmer slowly for 10 minutes. Remove cover and put aside to cool.
2. Meanwhile, put the crackers, paprika, thyme, and pepper in a plastic or paper bag, close, and crush with your hands to reduce the crackers to small pieces. Do not crush too fine; they should in no way resemble bread crumbs.
3. With the oil coat a 4- or 5-cup soufflé or similar dish, and scatter in about one-third of the crushed crackers. Pick over the oysters, pulling off any hard muscle pieces that may still be attached. (If the oysters are large, cut into 2 or 3 pieces.) Drop half the oysters over the bed of crackers. Scatter half the cooked celery and scallion mixture over them.
4. Make another layer with half the crackers left over and all the oysters and vegetables. Top with the remaining crackers. If the top layer of crackers does not completely cover the oysters, crush a few more and scatter them over the surface.

5. In a bowl or pitcher, combine ½ cup of the oyster liquor, the cream, and hot pepper sauce. Pour the mixture over the oyster-cracker layers. You should just be able to see the liquid; however, the top should not be covered with liquid. If there does not seem to be quite enough liquid, dribble on a few more tablespoons of the oyster liquor.
6. Bake for about 20 minutes, or until the surface is nicely browned and most of the liquid has been absorbed.
7. Using 2 serving spoons or tablespoons, serve at the table. Divide among 4 or 6 salad plates. Garnish with the bean salad or snow peas, if desired.

Serves 4 to 6.

HINT   If there is more oyster liquor than is called for, freeze it and use in fish soups and stews to replace water or bottled clam juice.

Mackerel Poached in White Wine

You can prepare the mackerel for this dish in several ways. First, you may prefer to keep it whole, because cooking the entire fish produces a more gelatinous and flavorful sauce. Second, if you do not like boning the fish yourself at the table, have the mackerel boned and the heads removed. The third and least preferred method is to cook only the fillets.

If you choose either of the latter two preparations, add the heads and bones to the cooking stock along with the rest of the fish, then carefully discard before serving.

This light but emphatically flavored dish is best when made a day or two ahead to allow the lemony seasoning to completely penetrate the fish. This dish should be served at room temperature.

PREPARATION TIME   10 minutes
COOLING TIME FOR COURT BOUILLON   1 hour
COOKING   30 minutes
MARINATING   24 hours

3½ cups Court Bouillon
(see page 28)
2 lemons, thinly sliced

6 medium-size mackerel, very firm and fresh, 4 to 5 ounces each

1. Place the Court Bouillon, including one of the thinly sliced lemons, in a nonreactive pot, cover, and simmer for 20 minutes. Cool completely.
2. Preheat oven to 350°F. Clean and rinse the mackerel and place in a deep baking dish. Pour the unstrained bouillon over the mackerel. The liquid should reach about one-half the depth of the fish; if not, add more white wine. If heads have been removed, or the fish filleted, tuck the heads and bones around the fish.
3. Place the baking dish on a heat deflecting pad (or metal trivet) over medium heat and bring the bouillon to a very slow simmer. Cover and place in the oven. Keep the liquid just at the simmering point and cook for 10 minutes or so, depending on the size of the mackerel. (Fillets take less time.) The fish is done when the flesh flakes easily when pierced with a fork. Remove from the oven and let the fish cool in the liquid, still covered, for about 1 hour. Remove bay leaf.

4. Refrigerate overnight. Before serving, remove the fish from refrigerator long enough in advance to remove the chill.
5. Whether serving on a large platter, or on individual dishes, carefully spoon some of the sauce over the fish. Garnish with the other thinly sliced lemon.

Serves 6.

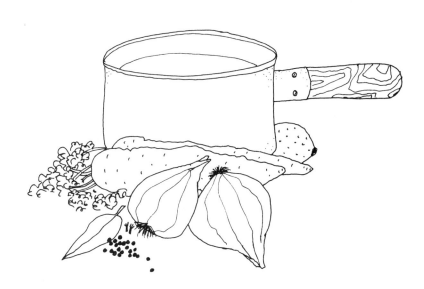

White-Capped Smokey Salmon

This is an unusual and tasty smoked salmon dish. The mild licorice note of the star anise is an essential part of its delicate flavor. The smokiness of the salmon contrasts nicely with the white glazing, which is cool at first taste, then ends with a snap. You can smoke the salmon a day or two in advance—the flavor will be even better.

PREPARATION TIME   7 minutes

COOKING   15 minutes

CHILLING   1 hour

Salt and pepper

2 tablespoons black tea leaves

2 tablespoons brown sugar

1 tablespoon juniper berries, crushed

1 bay leaf, broken in half

1 star anise*

1 to 1¼ pounds salmon fillets, or salmon trout

Oil

Sauce

¼ cup sour cream

¾ cup low-fat yogurt

¼ cup prepared horseradish

Salt and pepper

5 or 6 lettuce leaves

1 tomatillo, chopped (page 35) or ¼ cup snipped fresh chives

1. Smoke the salmon according to the directions for Quick-Smoked Trout Canapés (page 51), using all the flavoring ingredients in the smoking mixture. Smoke the salmon for only 10 minutes. (The fillet is thinner than the whole trout.) Remove from the heat and let stand 5 minutes before removing foil. Chill for at least 1 hour.
2. Meanwhile, make the sauce. Stir the sour cream, yogurt, and horseradish until well blended; season with several grindings of pepper and a pinch of salt and stir again.
3. Put the lettuce on 5 or 6 plates. Remove any bones from the salmon and cut the fillet into pieces for an equal number of portions. Arrange the salmon on the lettuce and glaze the fish by spreading about 1½ tablespoons of the horseradish sauce over the top of each serving. Sprinkle with the chopped tomatillo or chives. Pass the rest of the sauce separately.

Serves 5 or 6.

*Star anise is available in the Oriental sections of supermarkets or specialty food stores.

Grilled Smelts and Jalapeño

Some admirers compare the flavor of smelts, when especially fresh, to that of cucumbers. Smelts lend themselves admirably to interesting combinations, such as in this dish.

PREPARATION TIME   18 minutes, including boning
COOKING   1 minute

8 smelts, 5 to 6 inches long	3 tablespoons cornmeal
Salt and pepper	Oil
4 jalapeño peppers	4 lime wedges

1. Bone the smelts according to the directions on page 14, and cut completely through the tails so the fish will lie flat. Rinse, pat dry on paper towels, and sprinkle the flesh side with salt and pepper.
2. Prepare the jalapeños according to the directions on page 35. Cut them completely in half, then lay the halves flat, skin side up.
3. Just before grilling, lightly coat the smelts on both sides with the cornmeal. Pat the cornmeal into the flesh and skin. Select a large, heavy (preferably cast-iron) skillet and wipe with a teaspoon of the oil. Heat to quite hot, and put the smelts and the peppers in the skillet. (If the skillet is not large enough, cook in two batches.) Fry for about 30 seconds on each side, pressing down on the peppers with a spatula to char the skin a little.
4. Place 2 grilled smelts on each salad-size plate along with 2 jalapeño halves, and add a lime wedge. Serve at once. Each diner eats as much, or as little, of the fiery jalapeño as suits his or her taste.

Serves 4.

Tuna on a Shredded Nest

Lettuce is combined with bok choy in this recipe to increase the size of the vegetable "nest." This tuna dish, when served with potato salad, makes a complete, refreshing summer lunch.

PREPARATION TIME   25 minutes
COOKING   35 minutes
MARINATING   1 day

1½ pounds fresh tuna
2 tablespoons olive oil
1 medium onion, sliced
3 medium carrots, finely sliced
6 cloves garlic, smashed and
   chopped (page 36)

1 lemon, thinly sliced
½ head iceberg lettuce, shredded
½ head bok choy, finely sliced
Salt and pepper
1½ cups dry white wine
6 thin slices lemon for garnish

1. Rinse the tuna and pat dry. Select a tightly covered pot that will hold the tuna and vegetables snugly. Add the oil to the pot and heat until quite hot. Quickly sear the tuna on both sides and remove.
2. Add the onion and carrots to the oil remaining in the pot and sauté until lightly browned, about 7 minutes. Add the garlic and lemon slices and cook 30 seconds.
3. Remove half the vegetables and stir in half the shredded lettuce and bok choy. Replace the tuna and add any juices that may have accumulated. Top the fish with the remaining shredded greens, then scatter the sautéed vegetables on top. Pour in the wine and lightly salt and pepper the vegetables. Bring the wine to a simmer, place a piece of aluminum foil directly over the contents of the pot, then cover with the lid. Reduce the heat and simmer slowly for 20 minutes.
4. Remove the tuna and, to reduce and concentrate the juices, cook the contents in the pot over high heat for 5 minutes. Cool. Return the tuna, burying it under some vegetables, cover tightly, and refrigerate for at least 1 day.
5. Remove the tuna from the pot and cut into 6 portions. Stir all the vegetables together and make a nest of them in the center of the serving dishes. Place the tuna on top and spoon some reduced juices over the fish. Garnish with 6 thin lemon slices.

Serves 4 to 6.

Bluefish with Grapefruit Médaillon

Here you will find, in this unexpected pairing, a refreshing new dish. The tartness of the broiled grapefruit provides the perfect foil for the rich taste of the bluefish. Although one large grapefruit will serve six, the small end slices do not make an attractive base. So use two medium grapefruits and enjoy the leftover pieces for breakfast.

PREPARATION TIME   8 minutes
COOKING   15 to 20 minutes

1 pound fillet of bluefish, skin
    removed
1 tablespoon lime juice
1 tablespoon light soy sauce
1 teaspoon balsamic vinegar

1½ teaspoons ground cumin
2 medium grapefruits
1½ teaspoons sugar
1 tablespoon snipped fresh chives
½ tablespoon chopped pimiento

1. Place the bluefish on a large piece of plastic wrap. In a small bowl or cup, mix the lime juice, ½ tablespoon of the soy sauce, the vinegar, and ½ teaspoon of the cumin. Spread this sauce over the fish and tightly seal the fish within the plastic wrap. Wrap one more time for maximum protection. Steam (page 24) for at least 10 minutes; check and steam an extra 2 or 3 minutes if necessary. (For this recipe the bluefish must be thoroughly cooked.) Remove the package from the steamer and let it stand for 2 or 3 minutes before lifting the fish from the plastic wrap. When the plastic wrap can be handled, squeeze it to retrieve all its juices. Use 2 forks to flake the bluefish.
2. Preheat broiler. With a sharp, stainless steel knife, cut off both ends of each grapefruit. Stand the grapefruit up and, using vertical strokes, cut away the skin and white pith beneath it. Cut horizontally into ¼-inch slices and reserve 3 center slices from each of the grapefruits for this recipe. (Refrigerate the rest for another use.) In the small bowl or cup used for the bluefish sauce, mix together the remaining 1 teaspoon of cumin, the remaining ½ tablespoon soy sauce, and the sugar. On a baking sheet spoon this sauce over the grapefruit slices and broil for 4 or 5 minutes, or until the slices are nicely browned in a few areas.

3. Place a broiled grapefruit slice on a dish, top with bluefish, and spoon a little of the cooking juices over it. Sprinkle with chives and spoon a small mound of pimiento in the center. Serve hot or lukewarm.

Serves 6.

Mediterranean Marinated Shark

This is an unusually savory appetizer. The thick slices of shark are quickly fried, removed from the heat, and marinated in the hot sauce for a day or two. The result is a dish with a brisk and exhilarating flavor. Although suggested as a first course for a dinner party, it also makes a delicious main course at lunch or dinner.

The preservative qualities of the wine and vinegar help to keep this dish fresh for a few days, if stored in the refrigerator. Baste the fish every day to keep the top moist.

PREPARATION TIME   18 minutes

COOKING   20 minutes

CHILLING   24 hours

Sauce

1 cup Tomato Sauce
   (page 31)
½ cup red wine vinegar
½ cup dry white wine
¼ cup olive oil

1 teaspoon fresh rosemary or
   ½ teaspoon dried
1 teaspoon sugar
A pinch saffron
3 cloves garlic, peeled and chopped

Oil for frying
2 pounds shark, cod, or halibut,
   sliced 1 to 1½ inches thick

About ¾ cup flour
Salt and pepper

1. Put all sauce ingredients into a small pot, cover, and simmer for 20 minutes. While the sauce is simmering, pour oil in a skillet to a depth of about ½ inch and heat until very hot. Flour the fish slices and fry quickly in the oil; turn to brown both sides. Fry the fish 1 to 2 minutes per side, depending on thickness. Remove fried fish to a large deep heatproof dish, approximately 12 × 8 × 1½ inches. As you transfer the fish, drain off as much oil as possible before placing in the dish. Sprinkle with salt and pepper.
2. Pour the boiling sauce over the slices. Cover at once with plastic wrap, then with aluminum foil, and let cool to room temperature. Refrigerate at least 24 hours.

3. Remove fish from refrigerator 30 minutes before serving. Lift a slice of fish onto an individual dish and cover liberally with the sauce. Pass crusty French bread to absorb the extra sauce.

Serves 6 to 8 as a first course; 4 as a main course.

HINT   Leftover sauces can be used in many ways. In this case, poach bluefish fillets in the remaining sauce for about 10 minutes and serve hot. The acidic quality of the sauce balances the rich flavor of the bluefish.

Steamed Fish Steak Ceylon

This simple but pungent dish calls for only a few flavorings. Still, one sniff of the final aroma and the Orient immediately comes to mind. Serve the fish warm with cool, crisp lettuce.

PREPARATION TIME   8 minutes
MARINATING   15 minutes
COOKING   about 10 to 15 minutes

4 scallions
¾ pound skinless fish steak such
    as mahimahi, mako shark, or
    swordfish
1 tablespoon light soy
    sauce

1 teaspoon rice wine vinegar or
    mild wine vinegar
¼ teaspoon five-spice powder
4 lettuce leaves, preferably Boston
2 tablespoons chopped fresh
    cilantro leaves

1. Cut the scallions in half crosswise, then cut the white sections in half lengthwise. On the counter lay a piece of plastic wrap about twice the size of the fish steak, and place the fish in the center.
2. Mix the soy sauce, vinegar, and five-spice powder in a cup. Pour half the sauce over the fish, turn the steak, and pour the remaining sauce over it. Lay the scallions over the top and wrap snugly with the plastic wrap. Make certain that the seams are closed. Put aside to marinate for 15 minutes or longer, but no more than 1 hour. Turn the package over several times while marinating.
3. Place the fish package in a steamer, scallion side down, and steam for 10 to 15 minutes. Since you can see through the plastic, check to see if it is done to your likeness. (Some cooks prefer to keep the steak a little pink in the center.) If further cooking is desired, steam 2 or 3 minutes more.
4. Lift the fish package out of the steamer with a spatula and place on a dish. Slit the plastic wrap with scissors and remove; transfer the scallions to a small dish. A good deal of juice will be caught in the crevices of the plastic, which cools quickly. Squeeze the plastic over a plate to retain the juices.
5. Place a lettuce leaf on each of 4 plates, cut the fish, either into fingers or slices, and arrange on the lettuce. Garnish with the scallions,

cilantro leaves, and some of the marinade. The fish is meant to be eaten with all the elements of the presentation—lettuce, scallions, and cilantro. Steamed Fish Steak Ceylon does not have to be served hot; it is perhaps best served warm, or at room temperature.

Serves 4.

HINT   Five-spice powder is a blend of spices that usually includes star anise, Sichuan peppercorn, fennel or anise seed, clove, and Chinese cinnamon. It is generally sold in powdered form and will keep indefinitely in a covered jar at room temperature. Look for it in Oriental sections of the supermarket or in Oriental food stores. Home blends generally lack the authenticity of the premixed spices.

Seafood Terrine

Seafood terrines are considered to be among the significant achievements of grand cuisine. Once a laborious undertaking, terrines are now comparatively easy to make, thanks to the food processor. This recipe should encourage cooks who are still wary about making terrines—first, because it is easy; second, because this version reduces the amount of heavy cream that is traditionally used by two thirds; and third, the results are delectable and a perfect start of a special dinner. Terrines also make an excellent main course for a summer luncheon or a light dinner.

PREPARATION TIME   30 minutes
CHILLING   1 hour
COOKING   about 1½ hours
MATURING   2 days

1 cup water	1 tomato, peeled and seeded
¾ cup dry white wine	(page 34)
A 3-inch piece celery	3 slices soft white bread, crusts
¼ lemon	removed
¼ teaspoon salt	⅓ cup milk
A large pinch pepper	1 pound cod or flounder fillets, cut
¼ pound medium shrimp,	into 1-inch pieces
unpeeled	A few drops hot red pepper sauce
¼ pound bay scallops	3 egg whites
2 shallots, chopped	½ cup heavy cream
1 oil-packed anchovy fillet	Oil

1. In a small covered pot, boil the water, ¼ cup of the white wine, celery, juice of the lemon (toss in the shell of the lemon as well), and salt and pepper for 5 minutes. Add the shrimp, reduce the heat, cover, and cook for 1 minute. Remove the shrimp with a skimmer and cool under cold running water. Put shrimp aside while poaching the scallops in the same broth. Cook scallops for about 30 seconds (depending on their size), or until they begin to turn white and firm. Drain at once. Peel the shrimp and cut into ¼-inch pieces. If the scallops are large, cut them into ¼-inch pieces. Chill the shrimp and the scallops.
2. In a small 2-cup pot, rapidly boil the remaining ½ cup white wine and the shallots until only about 1 tablespoon of liquid remains. Add the

anchovy fillet, stir, and simmer until it dissolves. Transfer contents into a small cup or bowl, cool, then chill.

3. Put the tomato in a small sieve and press to extract as much juice as possible. Chill. Break the bread into pieces and put in a mixing bowl with the milk. Turn the bread so that it absorbs the milk.

4. Put the fish in the food processor and pulse several times. Add the milk-soaked bread, shallots with anchovy, tomato, hot pepper sauce, and salt and pepper and pulse several times. Scrape down the sides of the bowl and, with the motor running, add the egg whites. Scrape down the bowl and, with the motor running, pour in the cream. Poach a teaspoon of this mousseline mixture, cool slightly, and taste for seasoning.

5. Cut parchment or wax paper to fit the top and bottom of a 6-cup ceramic or glass mold. (A meatloaf dish is perfect.) Oil the mold, fit 1 paper piece in the bottom, and oil it. Stir the cooked shrimp and scallops into the mousseline and spoon into the mold, making certain it reaches into the corners. Tap the dish sharply on the counter several times to settle the mousseline into the mold. Smooth the surface and tap the mold again. Oil the remaining piece of paper, and place it, oiled side down, over the mousseline, and cover. If the mold does not have a lid, use a double thickness of heavy-duty foil, and cut a small slash into it.

6. Put the mold in a large baking dish containing enough hot water to reach half the depth of the mold. Bake for about 1½ hours, or until a thermometer registers 150°F. The terrine should feel firm to the touch. Leave mold in the water, remove the cover, and cool for 30 minutes. Remove the mold from the water. Refrigerate the terrine for at least 1 day; 2 days is even better.

7. Remove the terrine from the refrigerator about 1 hour before serving. Unmold onto a platter, removing both pieces of paper. Cut terrine into slices with a serrated knife, using a sawing motion. Serve slices on individual plates or a serving platter, garnished with a mixture of lettuce leaves and radicchio, or place slices on a bed of lettuce chiffonade (see page 34).

Serves 10–12.

HINT To firm the terrine for easier slicing, put some light weights on top of the loaf before refrigerating it. The weights should not exceed 2½ pounds. You can use another meatloaf dish partially filled with water, or heavy juice or soup cans. Refrigerate. Remove the weights after 3 hours.

CHAPTER THREE

Soups and Stews

BLUE MUSSEL

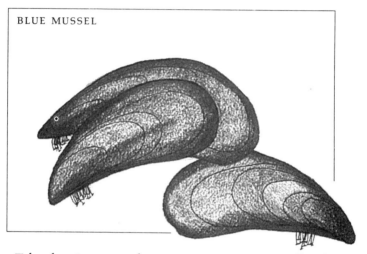

Take the time to make your own soup, especially if flavor, texture, and nutrition are important to you. Most prepared soups come loaded with sodium, plus a fair helping of saturated fats and preservatives. And the taste doesn't come close to the fresh, sparkling flavor of a homemade soup. If time is a factor, the blender or food processor is a great help.

The soups that follow offer a range from the very lightest, such as Squid in a Golden Consommé, to the more robust Fisherman's Chowder. Some of these soups are excellent introductions to a meal; others are complete meals in themselves. All are meant to be savored for their fresh goodness.

Corn and Crab Soup

Sometimes, with this type of soup, the purée is put through a sieve to remove the bits of corn kernel. However, because the rougher texture of the corn is satisfying on the palate and provides an agreeable base for the crab, that refining process has not been done here. To preserve the delicate flavor of the crab, use homemade chicken stock. If you must use canned broth, dilute it by a third with water.

You can prepare this soup through Step 2 of the recipe, then cool and refrigerate it. At serving time, bring the soup to a simmer and complete the recipe.

PREPARATION   15 minutes

COOKING   20 minutes

2 leeks

3 cups corn kernels, fresh or
   frozen (if frozen, use
   unbuttered variety)

1½ celery ribs, sliced

1 medium potato, peeled and
   diced

¾ cup dry white wine

¾ cup Chicken Stock (page 29)

¾ cup water

½ teaspoon sugar

¼ teaspoon anise seeds

1 soft lettuce leaf

3 to 3½ cups milk

1 teaspoon salt

A pinch ground pepper

A few drops hot red pepper sauce

½ pound lump or backfin crab,
   picked over

1. Clean the leeks according to the directions on page 201, then slice, white parts only. In a 2-quart nonreactive pot, put 2½ cups of the corn, leeks, celery, potato, white wine, Chicken Stock, water, and sugar. Place the anise seeds in the center of the lettuce leaf, fold over the lettuce to envelope the seeds, close with a toothpick, and add the lettuce package to the pot. Cover, bring to a simmer, and cook for 15 minutes. If the potatoes are completely cooked, remove the pot from the heat. Discard the lettuce package.

2. Ladle the vegetables and liquid into a food processor or blender and purée until smooth. (If using a blender, you'll have to do this in batches.) There should be about 2½ cups purée. Rinse out the cooking pot and pour the purée into it. Add the remaining ½ cup corn, 3 cups

of the milk, salt, pepper, and hot pepper sauce. Bring to a simmer, partially cover, and cook 5 minutes. If the soup seems too thick, add more milk until desired consistency is achieved. Keep in mind that the crabmeat will absorb some of the liquid.

3. Divide the crabmeat among 6 soup cups and top with the hot soup.

Serves 6 to 8.

HINT   A lettuce package is a handy way to add extra flavorings to simmering soups, stews, and stocks. The mild lettuce adds no flavor of its own, but its structure is such that the hot stock breaks down the membranes, allowing the liquid to wash through the herbs or spices inside and absorb their flavor. A lettuce package can be added and removed at any point during the cooking process.

Scallop Soup

This soup should be served warm, not boiling hot, because the subtle taste of creamed shellfish soups comes through better at lower temperatures.

The soup can be made in advance, covered, and refrigerated. Reheat before serving.

PREPARATION TIME   7 minutes
COOKING   35 minutes

1 quart water
⅔ cup dry white wine
1 tablespoon dry vermouth
2 scallions, white parts only, chopped
⅛ teaspoon saffron threads
⅛ teaspoon curry powder
¼ teaspoon dry mustard
1 medium potato, peeled and cut into chunks

½ teaspoon salt
½ teaspoon pepper
½ pound bay or sea scallops
¼ cup heavy cream or half-and-half
½ cup milk
1 teaspoon light soy sauce or ½ teaspoon regular soy sauce
Paprika and 6 parsley sprigs for garnish

1. Pour the water into a nonreactive pot and add the wine, vermouth, scallions, saffron, curry, mustard, potato pieces, salt, and pepper. Bring to a boil, cover, and simmer for 15 minutes. Add the scallops and simmer 2 to 4 minutes, depending on their size.
2. Purée the soup in a blender or food processor. (If using a blender, purée in 2 batches.) The scallops will not purée completely. Return the soup to the pot and add the cream, milk, and soy sauce. Reheat, but do not boil. Let stand, covered, for 10 to 15 minutes.
3. Ladle the creamed soup into cups or bowls. Make sure you stir the soup to include in each serving some of the scallop pieces, which will have sunk to the bottom. Dust with paprika and place a parsley sprig in the center of each serving.

Serves 6.

Scallops in Vegetable Broth

This tasty soup works as a main course because it contains an ample amount of scallops. The rest of the meal should be planned accordingly: perhaps a small pasta dish as an opener and a dessert of baked fruit, pastry, or a satiny mousse.

You can prepare the broth ahead of time, let it cool, and refrigerate it. Bring the soup back to a simmer near serving time, and add the scallops.

PREPARATION TIME 15 minutes
COOKING 30 minutes

2 leeks	½ teaspoon ground sage
4 carrots	½ teaspoon dried basil
1 small to medium onion	A pinch cayenne
1 celery rib	Salt to taste
12 cups water	1 teaspoon pepper
4 or 5 parsley sprigs, tied in a	1 cup dry vermouth
bundle	2 pounds bay or sea scallops,
1 teaspoon dried thyme	sliced in half crosswise if large

1. Clean the leeks according to the directions on page 201. Cut the white parts only into julienne (page 35). Also cut the carrots, onion, and celery into equally thin julienne. In a large pot, bring water to a boil and add the vegetables with parsley bundle, thyme, sage, basil, cayenne, salt, and pepper. Simmer for 15 minutes.
2. Add the vermouth and simmer for 10 minutes. Remove the parsley bundle.
3. Add the scallops and cook 2 to 3 minutes, depending on their size. Do not overcook.
4. Ladle the soup into individual soup bowls and serve at once.

Serves 6.

Green Goddess Scallop Soup

Green, leafy vegetables make up the base of this delicate soup, while potatoes add a bit of body. It is excellent served either hot or cold. If serving it chilled, you will find that the pearly white scallops darken a little. However, a dollop of sour cream or yogurt on top will add the needed sparkle.

PREPARATION TIME   15 minutes
COOKING   25 minutes

½ pound potatoes, peeled and diced
8 ounces spinach, washed and stemmed
4 ounces lettuce, preferably leaf or Romaine
3 scallions, chopped
½ cup chopped fresh parsley leaves (½ ounce)
½ teaspoon chopped fresh dill or ¼ teaspoon dried
2 cups water

¼ cup dry white wine
Salt and pepper
1½ cups milk
Few drops hot red pepper sauce
½ pound bay or sea scallops
¼ cup heavy cream (optional)
¼ cup shredded jicama, enoki mushrooms, snipped fresh chives, sour cream, or yogurt for garnish (optional)

1. Place the potatoes in the bottom of a deep, 8-quart nonreactive pot. Add the spinach, lettuce, scallions, parsley, dill, water, wine, and season lightly with salt and pepper. Place over medium heat, bring the liquid to a boil, cover, and cook for about 20 minutes, or until the potatoes are soft.
2. Purée the mixture in a food processor or blender until smooth. Rinse out the pot and pour the purée back into it. Stir in the milk and hot pepper sauce. Taste for seasonings and correct if necessary. Rinse the scallops. If using sea scallops, cut them in half crosswise.
3. Bring the soup to a simmer, add the scallops, and cook slowly for 1 or 2 minutes, depending on their size. Stir often and do not overcook. Remove from the heat and stir in the cream, if using. The cream will lighten the deep green color of the soup.

4. Ladle into individual soup cups, making certain each portion has an equal amount of scallops. Top with any of the optional garnishes. Serve at once, but this soup is equally good at a less-than-hot temperature.

Serves 5 or 6.

Oyster Soup

This rich-tasting soup is a variation on the standard oyster stew. Its flavors are deliciously subtle but not bland.

If a boiled or baked potato happens to be in the refrigerator, peel and use it instead of beginning with a raw one.

PREPARATION TIME   10 minutes
COOKING   20 minutes

1 large potato, peeled and cut into pieces
1 pint shucked oysters, standard size or smaller
1½ tablespoons butter or margarine
½ onion, coarsely chopped
1 celery rib, sliced
3 cups Fish Stock (page 27) or clam juice

1½ cups dry white wine
2 teaspoons anchovy paste
Cayenne to taste
Salt to taste
1 teaspoon grated lemon rind
¼ cup heavy cream or half-and-half
Paprika
¼ cup snipped fresh chives

1. Boil the potato until soft. Drain. Put the oysters and their liquor in a 2- or 3-quart nonreactive soup pot over medium heat. As soon as the liquor begins to simmer and the oysters' edges curl, remove the pot from the heat. Gently stir the oysters, then remove them with a skimmer. Strain the liquor through fine cheesecloth or a damp dish towel into a bowl.
2. Rinse out the oyster pot and lightly wipe it. Melt the butter or margarine in the pot and add the onion and celery. Cover and cook for 5 minutes. Add the Fish Stock, wine, strained oyster liquor, anchovy paste, cayenne, salt, and the cooked potato. Bring to a boil and simmer 10 minutes, uncovered. While the soup is cooking, remove the hard piece of muscle that may be attached to the oysters and discard.
3. Purée the vegetables and the broth mixture in a food processor or blender. Rinse out the pot, return the purée to the pot, and bring to a simmer. Add the oysters. Stir briefly, just long enough to heat them. Remove from the heat and stir in the grated lemon rind and the cream.
4. Ladle the soup and oysters into 6 bowls and garnish with a dusting of paprika and the chives.

Serves 6.

Squid in a Golden Consommé

This elegant soup is a perfect start to a festive dinner. The white, satiny rings of squid float in a pale yellow broth. The flavor is intriguing and indefinable.

The consommé can be clarified and refrigerated the day before and reheated at serving time. The squid, too, can be cooked the day before, but not sliced, and refrigerated separately; remove from the refrigerator an hour before serving and slice.

PREPARATION TIME   25 minutes
COOKING   about 5 minutes

1 squid, cleaned (page 19)
One 28-ounce can whole
  tomatoes
2 cups clam juice

1 tablespoon lemon juice
A pinch freshly ground pepper
1 egg white and the egg shell
2 tablespoons water

1. Pass the tomatoes through a food mill to purée them. (Do not use a blender or food processor for this; the super-fast action of those machines turns the tomatoes pink and frothy.) Pour the tomato purée and clam juice into a 2-quart nonreactive pot. Season with the lemon juice and pepper.
2. In a small bowl, beat the egg white and water together until they become a little frothy, and scrape them into the pot. Crush the egg shell and toss it in, too. Put the pot on medium heat, and whisking almost continuously, bring to a boil. Do not heat the soup too fast, as the egg white must have time to coagulate and absorb all the solid bits in the liquid. Once the egg whites have floated to the top and the liquid has come to a simmer, watch carefully. There will be a thick layer of froth on top and when it "cracks," turn off the heat. Let the soup stand for a few minutes.
3. To clarify the consommé, line a colander with a wet dish towel and suspend it over a bowl. (The bowl should be deep enough so that the bottom of the colander does not touch it.) Ladle the soup and egg white into the colander and allow the soup to drain into the bowl.

Remove the colander and discard the coagulated egg white and shells. What remains in the bowl is a crystal clear consommé.

4. Bring 1 quart of salted water to a boil, add the squid, and poach for 1 to 2 minutes, or just until the body turns opaque white. *Do not overcook.* Drain and cool at once under cold running water. (This extra step of poaching the squid can be eliminated by putting the raw squid rings into the soup cups and pouring the hot consommé over them. However, some of the clarity of the soup will be sacrificed.) Pat the squid dry and cut it into thin rings.

5. Ladle the consommé into soup bowls or cups and garnish with 3 or 4 squid rings.

Serves 4.

HINT Any stock or liquid can be clarified using this egg-white technique. The egg-white globules disperse throughout the stock and absorb all the minute floating solids and cloudy particles. Professional chefs toss in crumbled egg shells as well because the skin that clings to the inside of the shell helps to further clarify the soup.

Cold Salmon Soup

This is a crystal clear, very pretty cold soup, ideal as the first course of a summer meal. Because some flavor is always lost during the clarification process, bottled clam juice can be used here without a great difference in the flavor. However, you may want to use Fish Stock, if only for its fresh delicacy.

Since this is a chilled soup, everything, except the spinach, can be prepared ahead of time. Blanch the spinach an hour or so before serving.

PREPARATION TIME   20 minutes
COOKING   20 minutes
CHILLING   2 hours

¼ pound salmon fillet
Salt and pepper
3 cups Fish Stock (page 27) or
clam juice
2 teaspoons chopped fresh dill or 1
teaspoon dried
1 teaspoon fennel seeds

1 teaspoon anise-flavored liqueur,
or to taste
1 tablespoon lemon juice
1 egg white and egg shell
2 tablespoons water
3 or 4 spinach leaves, washed and
stemmed

1. Put the salmon in a heatproof pan that will hold it snugly. Lightly sprinkle with salt and pepper and pour 1 or more cups of the stock over the salmon. (The fish should be almost completely immersed.) Cover the pan and place on medium-low heat. Slowly bring the stock to a simmer and poach very gently for 10 minutes. To keep the salmon flesh moist and tender, it must be poached slowly. Remove the cover; if there is an undercooked spot on the top, turn the fillet over in the hot stock and put aside for a minute, off the heat. Remove at once to a plate, cool, and chill.
2. While the salmon is poaching, simmer the Fish Stock in a nonreactive pot with the dill, fennel seeds, liqueur, and lemon juice. Bring to a simmer, cover, and cook for 10 minutes. Once the salmon has been poached, add its stock to the seasoned stock, along with any juices that have collected in the salmon dish. Taste for seasonings.

3. Clarify the broth according to the directions in the preceding recipe. Cool, then chill.
4. Roll the spinach leaves into a tight cylinder and cut into chiffonade (page 34). Place the strips in a colander and pour boiling water over them, just enough to wilt them. Immediately cool under cold running water and squeeze dry. Refrigerate.
5. Before serving, flake the salmon. Divide the spinach among 4 soup cups and top with some of the salmon. (The presentation should look delicate; there should not be an overwhelming amount of either spinach or salmon.) Ladle the cold salmon broth over the garnishes.

Serves 4.

Mussels Provençale

This main dish soup is easy to make, inexpensive, and extremely good. Some readers may be puzzled by the instruction to pierce the pieces of orange rind with a toothpick. The toothpick allows for easy retrieval if the orange flavor seems too intense. The rind must be removed before serving the soup, anyway. Don't be startled at the addition of gin. Its juniper berry flavor has a great affinity with mussels, and the alcohol evaporates in the cooking.

The basic broth can be prepared in advance, even the day before, and refrigerated. The mussels, of course, must be cooked at the last minute.

PREPARATION TIME   15 minutes
COOKING   30 minutes

2 tablespoons olive oil	1 small piece orange rind, speared
1 medium onion, chopped	on a toothpick
¼ cup chopped celery, or 1	½ bay leaf
teaspoon celery seeds	½ teaspoon anchovy paste
1 clove garlic, peeled and minced	½ cup dry white wine
2 cups chopped fresh tomatoes, or	1 teaspoon salt
one 1-pound can plum tomatoes	½ teaspoon freshly ground pepper
1 teaspoon fennel seeds	2 tablespoons gin
1 teaspoon chopped basil,	2 pounds mussels, scrubbed and
preferably fresh	cleaned (page 17)

1. In a deep, heavy stovetop casserole, heat the oil over medium heat, then add the onion and celery. (If using celery seeds, add them later.) Stir the vegetables, cover, and simmer for 5 minutes. Add the garlic and cook for 1 minute.
2. Add the celery seeds and all the remaining ingredients, except the gin and mussels. Stir well, cover, and cook over medium-low heat for 20 minutes. After about 5 minutes of cooking, taste the sauce; if the orange flavor is too pronounced, remove the piece of rind, otherwise remove the bay leaf and orange rind at the end of the cooking time.
3. Turn the heat to high, add the gin, and stir. Immediately add the mussels, cover, and cook for about 3 minutes, or until the shells open.

Stir once or twice with a long-handled spoon to rearrange the mussels.

4. Using a skimmer, divide the mussels among 4 deep bowls, discarding any mussels that have not opened. Ladle the tomato broth over the mussels and serve at once. Provide plenty of paper napkins and a large bowl for the discarded shells.

Serves 4 as a main course.

One-Pot Clam Chowder

There are many, many versions of New England clam chowder. Although salt pork is traditional in this flavorful version, bacon contributes a smokier taste; use Canadian bacon or smoked turkey breast, if you prefer. Do not strain the clam liquor through cheesecloth, which tends to be flimsy and porous; use a clean dish towel instead.

The chowder can be completed through Step 4, cooled, and refrigerated.

PREPARATION TIME   20 minutes
COOKING   35 minutes

18 hard-shell clams, cherrystone
   or littleneck (about 4 pounds)
1 cup water
2 ounces bacon (about 2 slices),
   rind removed and cut into
   pieces (or Canadian bacon or
   smoked turkey breast, cut into
   pieces)
1 medium onion, chopped

1 celery rib, sliced
2 large potatoes (about 1 pound),
   peeled and diced
1 to 1½ cups clam juice
½ cup light cream
1½ cups milk
Pepper to taste
Cayenne to taste

1. Scrub the clams well and put them in a heavy, preferably enameled, cast-iron casserole with a 4- to 5-quart capacity. Pour in the water, cover, and place over high heat. As soon as the clams begin to open, about 6 minutes, remove the pot from the heat. With a skimmer transfer the clams to a bowl. Wet a dish towel and use it to line a colander set over a deep mixing bowl. Carefully pour the clam juice into the colander, stopping before you pour in the sand at the bottom. Measure the strained liquor and reserve.
2. Rinse the pot, wipe with a paper towel, and place over medium heat. Add the bacon and slowly fry the pieces until well browned and crisp. With the skimmer transfer the bacon to paper towels to drain. Pour off all but 2 tablespoons of the fat.
3. Add the onion and celery to the pot, cover, and sauté for about 3 minutes. Add the potatoes. Add enough bottled clam juice to the

strained liquor to measure 3 cups and pour over the vegetables. Cover and simmer for 15 minutes, or until the potatoes are soft.

4. While the chowder is cooking, remove the clams from their shells, discarding any that do not open. Slice the clams, if you like, but do not chop into bits. Divide the clams among 4 or 5 chowder bowls.

5. Return the bacon to the pot, add the light cream, milk, and pepper, and cook 5 minutes. If the chowder seems too thick, pour in some extra clam juice.

6. Ladle the super-hot chowder over the clams, sprinkle with a little cayenne, and serve at once.

Serves 4 or 5.

HINT   Cooked clams will stay fresh for a few days if they're stored in a tightly closed container. A tablespoon or two of clam juice sprinkled over them will prevent them from drying out.

Thon à la Bordelaise

(TUNA AND RED WINE STEW)

Tuna's dark meat and deep flavor combine beautifully with the red wine and beef stock in this savory main dish stew. Serve with a pasta or rice accompaniment to absorb the sauce.

PREPARATION TIME   16 minutes
COOKING   45 minutes

¼ cup peanut oil
1 medium onion, chopped
3 tablespoons flour
2 cups dry red wine
1 cup Beef Stock (pages 29–30) or
  canned beef broth
3 shallots, finely chopped
3 cloves garlic, peeled and finely
  chopped
2 tablespoons tomato paste
Salt and pepper to taste

2 pounds tuna steak, preferably in
  1 piece
4 parsley sprigs
1 bay leaf
18 small white onions, peeled
4 fresh tomatoes, peeled and cut
  into thick wedges (page 34)
½ pound fresh mushrooms, cut in
  halves or quarters
Few drops brandy (optional)

1. Preheat oven to 325°F. Heat the oil in a 4- or 5-quart ovenproof casserole or pot. Add the chopped onion and cook slowly for about 5 minutes, stirring often to prevent browning. Add the flour, stirring well with a wire whisk, and cook for a few minutes. Slowly pour in the red wine and the beef stock, whisking constantly. When thoroughly blended, add the shallots, garlic, tomato paste, and salt and pepper. Simmer for 10 minutes.
2. Add the tuna, parsley, and bay leaf. Spoon some of the sauce over the tuna. Add additional red wine or Beef Stock if the sauce does not cover half the thickness of the tuna steak. Cover and put in the oven.
3. When the tuna has baked for 10 minutes, remove the parsley and bay leaf from the sauce and add the small white onions. Cook for 10 minutes, then add the tomatoes and mushrooms, and cook for 5 minutes.
4. When the tuna is done, remove it carefully to a heated platter. (The fish is delicate and breaks easily; it is best to use a spatula for

transferring.) If desired, add a few drops of brandy to the sauce and boil it down rapidly to reduce and thicken it.

5. Spoon the sauce and vegetables around the tuna. Pass the sauce separately.

Serves 6.

HINT   When only a small amount of tomato paste is used in a recipe, transfer the remaining paste into a small covered container and freeze it. Remove from the freezer about 10 minutes before needed and scoop out, with a hot teaspoon, as much as you require. The sugar content of the concentrated tomatoes prevents the paste from freezing rock solid, and it will keep for a few months.

Fisherman's Chowder

This is an easy-to-make, rich, and flavorful soup. For a simple and completely satisfying meal, serve it with crusty bread, a salad, and cheese.

PREPARATION TIME   15 minutes
COOKING   35 minutes

4 cloves garlic, peeled and sliced
¼ cup olive oil
1 large onion, chopped
3 celery ribs, sliced
One 28-ounce can plum tomatoes
1½ cups Fish Stock (page 27) or
  clam juice
2 cups water
¼ teaspoon dried rosemary
¼ teaspoon dried thyme
¼ teaspoon dried oregano
¼ teaspoon ground cumin

2 teaspoons anchovy paste
Few drops hot red pepper
  sauce
2 teaspoons light soy sauce
3 ounces (1 cup) very thin
  spaghetti (vermicelli), broken
  into small pieces
¼ teaspoon salt
⅛ teaspoon pepper
½ pound boneless fillet, such as
  pollock, turbot, or haddock, cut
  into ½-inch pieces

1. In a 4-quart soup pot or casserole, slowly brown the garlic in the oil; do not let it burn. Use a skimmer to remove the garlic and discard. Add the onion and celery to the pot, cover, and cook slowly for 5 minutes, or until the vegetables are slightly limp. Add the tomatoes, Fish Stock, water, rosemary, thyme, oregano, cumin, and anchovy paste, and simmer for 15 minutes, covered.
2. Add the hot pepper sauce, soy sauce, vermicelli, salt, and pepper. Cook 5 minutes. Add the fish pieces and cook, uncovered, for about 10 minutes. As the fish cooks, break up the pieces by mashing them against the sides of the pot with the back of a fork. Taste for seasoning and correct if necessary.
3. Ladle the soup into bowls.

Serves 6 to 8.

HINT   Remove the skin from a fish before cutting the fish into pieces. Add the skin to the soup pot to intensify the briny flavor, if desired, and discard it before serving.

Curried Cod Chowder

In some chowder recipes the potatoes are cooked with the other ingredients. But it's best to boil them separately for this recipe; the potato pieces add a mellow counterpoint to the pungent flavor of the curry in this hearty soup. If you like, cooked peas can also be added at the end.

The soup base can be prepared in advance, even a day ahead, and refrigerated. Remove the bay leaf and cloves before storing. At serving time, bring the base back to a simmer and add the fish and the cooked potatoes.

PREPARATION TIME   12 minutes

COOKING   35 minutes

2 medium waxy potatoes (1¼ to
   1½ pounds), scrubbed
2 tablespoons butter or margarine
2 celery ribs, sliced
6 scallions, sliced
3 tablespoons flour
2 teaspoons curry powder, or to
   taste
2 cups milk
2 cups Fish Stock (page 27) or
   clam juice

2 cups water
1 tablespoon light soy sauce
1 medium bay leaf
2 whole cloves
Salt and pepper
1½ pounds cod fillets, or monkfish
   or haddock, cut into 2-inch
   pieces
¼ cup light cream or half-and-
   half
Paprika

1. Boil the potatoes for 20 to 25 minutes, or until soft. Cool, peel, and cut into 1-inch chunks.
2. Meanwhile, melt the butter or margarine in a heavy 4-quart pot, add the celery and scallions, cover, and sauté for 5 minutes.
3. Add the flour and curry and stir with a whisk to make a roux—a thick paste that forms the base of the sauce. Cook for about 2 minutes. Slowly add the milk, whisking constantly to keep the mixture smooth. Pour in the Fish Stock and water, then add the soy sauce, bay leaf, cloves, and salt and pepper. Bring to a simmer, partially cover, and cook for 15 minutes.

4. With a skimmer, remove the bay leaf and cloves and discard. Add the fish pieces and potatoes and cook 2 or 3 minutes, or until the fish flakes easily. Remove from the heat and stir in the cream.
5. Ladle the soup into deep bowls and dust with paprika.

Serves 6.

Catfish Gumbo

Catfish is the preferred fish for this spicy gumbo. It has a deep, sweet flavor that holds up well to the strong seasonings. If fresh okra is not available, you can substitute frozen. Buy the whole frozen okra and slice it while still slightly frozen and firm.

PREPARATION TIME   15 minutes
COOKING   45 minutes

3 tablespoons olive oil
1 celery rib, chopped (about ½ cup)
½ green pepper, chopped (about ½ cup)
1 medium onion, chopped (about 1 cup)
2 cloves garlic, peeled and chopped
2 cups tomatoes, peeled and chopped (page 34), or one 1-pound can plum tomatoes

2 cups Beef Stock (pages 29–30)
¼ pound okra, sliced (about ½ cup)
1 small bay leaf
½ teaspoon dried thyme
½ teaspoon dried oregano
½ to ¾ teaspoon fennel seeds
¼ teaspoon cayenne
½ teaspoon salt
2 catfish fillets (about ¾ pound), or cod if catfish is not available
4 cups cooked unsalted rice

1. Heat the oil in a heavy nonreactive 4- or 5-quart pot. Add the celery, green pepper, and onion, cover, and cook slowly for 5 minutes. Add the garlic and cook, stirring, for 1 minute.
2. Add the tomatoes; if using canned tomatoes, crush them with your hands or a spoon as you add them to the pot. Add the Beef Stock. Add the okra and the bay leaf, thyme, oregano, fennel seeds, cayenne, and salt. Bring to a boil, cover, and simmer slowly for 30 minutes.
3. Cut the catfish fillets into 1-inch pieces. Remove the bay leaf. Stir the fish into the simmering gumbo and cook for another 7 minutes, or until the fish is cooked through.
4. Mound a cup of rice into each soup bowl and ladle the hot gumbo over it.

Serves 4.

CHAPTER FOUR

Main Courses

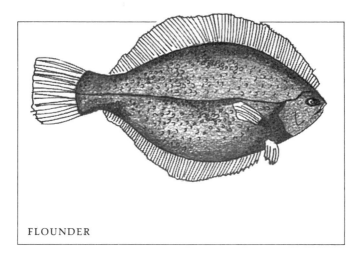

FLOUNDER

Here is where fish, in all its many varieties and
combinations, comes into its full glory—as the
centerpiece of the meal. In this chapter you will find
recipes for the traditional favorites, as well as
suggestions for preparing and serving lesser-known
varieties, such as monkfish, grouper, shark, blowfish,
and smelt. There are many delicious and simple
recipes for shellfish and mollusks, too.

Although main dish recipes are also found in other
chapters of this book, a greater diversity of fish and
of cooking methods and techniques is featured here;
the presentations range from the simple to the
elegant and showy.

Simple Fish Sauté

One of the easiest and fastest ways to prepare fish fillets is to do a quick sauté. The French name for this procedure is *à la meunière*, "in the style of the miller's wife." The miller's wife would have had plenty of flour on hand; so that is the coating given to the fillets. It is also important to select a pan that will hold the fish snugly. If necessary, fry the fillets in batches, either using two frying pans or quickly rinsing and wiping out the pan before beginning again. Don't overcook the fish—sautéing takes only a few minutes for each side.

This dish is excellent when served with succotash flavored with fresh snipped chives.

PREPARATION TIME   2 minutes
COOKING   about 5 minutes

4 fish fillets, such as sole,
  flounder, trout, or perch,
  preferably less than
  ½-inch thick
Salt and pepper to taste
Flour

2 tablespoons butter or
  margarine
2 tablespoons oil
1 lemon, cut into quarters
Fresh parsley for garnish

1. Rinse the fillets and dry on paper towels; sprinkle with salt and pepper. Spread the flour in a dish or on waxed paper. Dip each fillet into the flour, coating both sides thoroughly.
2. In a heavy skillet, melt the butter with the oil over fairly high heat. (If frying in 2 batches, use only half the oil and butter.) When the oil is hot and the butter foaming, put in the fish fillets. Reduce the heat to moderately high and sauté the fillets for about 3 minutes, or until they're a nice golden brown on the underside.
3. Turn the fillets over and sauté the other side until also a golden brown (about another 2 minutes).
4. Transfer the sautéed fillets to warm serving dishes. Garnish with a lemon wedge and some parsley.

Serves 4.

HINT   If the fillets are quite thick, reduce the heat to medium so that it will have time to penetrate through the flesh before the coating burns.

Crispy Baked Fish Fillets

Here is an excellent alternative to frying fish—one that uses a minimum amount of fat. Preparation is simple and quick, and the delicate flavor of the fish comes through nicely.

The fish can be completely prepared ahead of time. After breading, allow the fish to dry for 15 minutes, then refrigerate until 30 minutes before baking. Give the fish a few extra minutes in the oven if you take it directly from the refrigerator to the oven.

Since the oven is very hot, you can bake some tomato halves, seasoned with fresh basil and a little olive oil, simultaneously with the fish.

PREPARATION TIME   12 minutes
DRYING   15 minutes
BAKING   about 12 minutes

2 teaspoons oil	½ teaspoon dried oregano
6 fish fillets, such as sole, baby	½ cup low-fat milk
halibut, or flounder	1½ tablespoons butter or
1 cup bread crumbs	margarine
¼ teaspoon pepper	Paprika
3 tablespoons chopped fresh parsley	6 lemon wedges

1. Oil a baking dish that will hold the fillets flat. Rinse the fillets and dry them on paper towels. Spread the crumbs on a large piece of wax paper, add the pepper, parsley, and oregano, and toss to mix well.
2. Pour the milk into a dish. Dip the fillets on both sides into the milk, shake off the excess, then dip the fillets into the bread crumbs. Pat the crumbs well onto both sides of the fish and place fillets in the baking dish. Let stand to dry for at least 15 minutes. Meanwhile, preheat oven to 450°F.
3. Just before baking the fish, melt the butter or margarine and drizzle it over the fillets. Bake the fish for about 10 to 15 minutes; exact timing will depend on the thickness of the fillets. Test by piercing with a toothpick: the flesh should be white and firm. Sprinkle the paprika over the fillets for the last minute of baking.
4. Serve the fish directly from the baking dish, accompanied by lemon wedges.

Serves 6.

Fish Fillets en Papillotes

Traditionally, fish served *en papillote* is enclosed in parchment paper that browns and puffs up dramatically in the oven. Many people now substitute aluminum foil, which is perfectly acceptable, but lacks glamor. A happy compromise is the plastic oven bag—it's clear, puffs up, and lets you see what is going on inside. The results are flavorful, tender, and aromatic. Steamed carrot slices make a colorful addition to this dish.

PREPARATION TIME 10 minutes

COOKING 12 minutes

2 teaspoons butter or margarine, softened

1½ teaspoons prepared mustard

½ teaspoon minced garlic

½ lemon

½ cup chopped fresh parsley

Salt and pepper to taste

4 flounder or sole fillets, each about 4 ounces

1. Preheat oven to 375°F. Cream the butter or margarine, mustard, garlic, and 2 teaspoons of lemon juice. Mix in the parsley.
2. Rinse the fillets and dry them on paper towels. Gently rub both sides of each fillet with the lemon half and sprinkle with salt and pepper. Place 1 fillet on a board or large dish, skin side (the darker side) down. Spread half the flavored butter over the entire length of the fillet. Cover with another fillet, skin side up. Layer the remaining fillets in the same manner.
3. Slip the fillets into the baking bag and close tightly. (Follow manufacturer's instructions for preparing the bag.) Place the bagged fish on a baking sheet and bake for 10 to 15 minutes, depending on the thickness of the fillets. Test with a knife to see if the flesh flakes, indicating it is done.
4. Transfer the baking bag to a platter. Remove the closure and cut the bag open. Slice each pair of fillets in half and place on serving dishes. Spoon some of the cooking juices over the fish. Serve at once.

Serves 4.

HINT Lemon has many virtues, including the capacity to neutralize certain smells. To remove any odor of fish on your cutting board or hands, rub with the cut end of a lemon.

Fish Fillets Kowloon

A friend from Kowloon, one of Hong Kong's two main sections, has provided this simple, delicious recipe. She is a good cook who loves to entertain, and this dish is one of her specialties.

A green vegetable is the accompaniment of choice for this dish — string beans, asparagus, or broccoli.

PREPARATION TIME   2 minutes
COOKING   about 2 to 3 minutes

4 fish fillets, such as
    turbot, sole, flounder, or
    baby halibut, each about 5
    ounces
Salt and pepper

3 tablespoons dry sherry or white
    wine
3 tablespoons oil
1½ tablespoons light soy sauce
3 scallions, thinly sliced

1. Place the fillets in a dish and sprinkle with the salt and pepper and sherry. Place the dish on a trivet in a wok or another pot that contains an inch or so of water. Cover, and steam for about 2 to 3 minutes, or until the flesh is white and flakes easily. Precise timing will depend on the thickness of the fish.
2. While the fish is steaming, pour the oil and soy sauce into a small pot or butter-melter and heat, bringing almost to the boiling point.
3. Remove the dish from the steamer and strew the scallions over the fillets. Remove the small pot from the heat, stir the sauce a few times to blend the oil and soy sauce, and pour over the fillets. Serve at once.

Serves 4.

HINT   If you don't have a wok or suitable pot for steaming fish fillets, place each fillet on a piece of plastic wrap large enough to fit around the fish. Season with salt, pepper, and sherry, and fold over the plastic wrap, making a complete seal. Steam in a steamer or in boiling water in a large skillet. Timing will be the same as in a wok or pot — about 2 minutes. Remove with a slotted spoon or spatula.

Turban-Wrapped Fillets of Sole

The few minutes you spend in rolling these stuffed fillets into a tight turban pays off handsomely at the table. First of all, they make an impressive presentation. More important, the compact fish cooks more slowly and has less chance of being overdone. The fish turn out tender and flavorful, ready to be crowned with a delicious sauce.

The fillets can be stuffed and prepared for cooking a few hours in advance. Refrigerate until ready to use.

Wild rice, or a combination of white and wild rice, presents a nice contrast to the fish—and helps absorb the extra sauce.

PREPARATION TIME   15 minutes

SOAKING   15 minutes

COOKING   30 minutes

1 cup water
2 ounces dried mushrooms
1 tablespoon butter or margarine
2 tablespoons chopped shallots
4 ounces fresh mushrooms, thinly sliced
1/4 teaspoon dried tarragon
2 tablespoons chopped fresh parsley

1 tablespoon heavy cream
4 fillets of sole or flounder, each about 4 ounces
1/2 lemon
Salt and pepper
2 tablespoons dry vermouth
2 tablespoons dry white wine
1/2 teaspoon cornstarch

1. Bring the water to a boil and pour it over the dried mushrooms in a small bowl; cover and set aside for 15 minutes. Drain and reserve the liquid. Chop the soaked mushrooms (there should be about 1/4 cup).
2. Melt the butter or margarine in a 1-quart saucepan, add the shallots, cover, and sauté for 1 minute. Add the fresh mushrooms and tarragon, cover, and cook an additional 2 minutes. Remove the saucepan from the heat and stir in the parsley, cream, and chopped dried mushrooms.
3. Rinse the sole fillets and dry on paper towels. Rub each fillet on both sides with the lemon. Lay the fillets on the counter, skin side up (the darker side). Sprinkle lightly with salt and pepper. Spread one-fourth of the mushroom filling over each fillet. (Do not extend the filling to the very ends.) Roll up each fillet and secure the closing with a toothpick.

4. Select a heavy nonreactive pot that will hold the 4 rolled fillets snugly. Stand the "turbans" in the pot and pour the wines and ½ cup of the reserved mushroom soaking liquid over them. Put a piece of aluminum foil directly over the fillets, tucking it down inside the pot, then cover. Put the pot over a very low flame to heat the liquid gently. (Check from time to time to make certain that the liquid is not boiling.) The "turbans" should be poached in about 10 to 15 minutes maximum, and are done when the flesh is white and flakes easily. Carefully remove the rolled fillets to a warm serving platter, remove the toothpicks, and keep warm.
5. Boil the cooking liquid briskly for 5 minutes to reduce. Mix the cornstarch with a little water to make a paste, stir it into the simmering liquid, and cook 3 minutes.
6. Place a "turban" on each of 4 warm plates, drizzle a few tablespoons of sauce over each, and pass the remaining sauce in a sauceboat. Serve at once.

Serves 4.

HINT   Restaurant chefs often wipe the edge of each serving plate with a clean dish towel or paper towel before it is presented at the dining table. This final touch removes any spots, adds a little shine to the plate, and enhances the appearance of the food.

Mustard-Glazed Pollock

Anytime you see pollock, buy it. It costs about half as much as cod or haddock, which it resembles closely in texture and taste. When raw, its flesh is a little gray, but it cooks to a pristine white. Its appearance is also improved by a topping, and a mustard sauce is a delicious choice. Serve it with a mild vegetable, such as carrot purée or steamed zucchini.

PREPARATION TIME   6 minutes

COOKING   about 10 minutes

1½ pounds pollock fillets, or cod
   or haddock fillets
½ tablespoon oil
Salt and pepper

⅔ cup mayonnaise
3 tablespoons Dijon-style mustard
   (nongrainy)
1 tablespoon brandy

1. Preheat oven to 375°F. Run your fingers over the fish and remove any bones. Cut the fillet into 4 pieces, rinse, and pat dry. Oil a baking dish that will hold the fish comfortably without crowding. Arrange the fish in a single layer and sprinkle lightly with salt and pepper.
2. In a small bowl, mix the mayonnaise, mustard, brandy, salt, and pepper to taste. Spread the glaze over the fish and place the dish in the oven. Bake for 7 minutes, then check for doneness. Add an extra 3 to 5 minutes of cooking time if fillets are thick. Do not overbake.
3. Place under the broiler for 1 minute to give a nice glaze to the top. Serve at once.

Serves 4.

HINT   Keep a pair of tweezers in the kitchen drawer. You can grasp and extract fish bones much more quickly and easily with them than with your fingers.

Grouper with Red Onion Sauce

Although the vivid color of the red onions in this sauce fades somewhat during cooking, its rich flavor is right on target. Serve with rice or spaghetti.

The sauce can be completed the day before and refrigerated. Be sure to remove the bay leaf.

PREPARATION TIME 5 minutes
COOKING 1 hour

2 tablespoons vegetable oil
2 red onions, thinly sliced (¾ to 1 pound)
1 clove garlic, peeled and finely chopped
1 cup dry red wine
1 cup Fish Stock (page 27)
1 bay leaf
⅛ teaspoon dried thyme
Salt and pepper
1¼ pounds skinless grouper fillets
1 tablespoon flour
2 tablespoons heavy cream or half-and-half
2 tablespoons chopped fresh parsley

1. Heat the oil in a heavy nonreactive stovetop casserole and add the onions. Stir to coat the onions with the oil, cover, and cook gently for 20 minutes. Add the garlic and cook, stirring, for 1 minute.
2. Add the red wine, Fish Stock, bay leaf, thyme, and salt and pepper to taste. Cover and cook the sauce 20 minutes. Remove the bay leaf.
3. Meanwhile, cut the grouper into ½-inch-thick strips. When the sauce is ready, carefully put in the grouper slices, spoon some of the sauce over them, cover, and cook *very* slowly for 10 to 15 minutes. Check for doneness after 10 minutes.
4. Remove the fish from the casserole and keep warm. Increase the heat under the casserole to high and boil the sauce rapidly to reduce it by half.
5. Stir together the flour and cream. When the sauce is ready, reduce the heat to low, stir in the flour-cream mixture, and cook slowly for about 1 minute; do not boil. Return the grouper to the casserole, spoon some sauce over it, cover, and reheat for 1 or 2 minutes.
6. Spoon the grouper and red onion sauce in the center of a platter and surround with rice or spaghetti. Garnish with the chopped parsley.

Serves 4.

Codfish Fricassee

Corn makes an excellent accompaniment to this dish. Its bright yellow color and sweet flavor accent the robust taste of the red pepper sauce.

PREPARATION TIME   15 minutes

COOKING   25 minutes

2 tablespoons olive oil

2 sweet red peppers (about 1 pound), thinly sliced

1 medium onion, thinly sliced (about 1 cup)

¼ cup dry white wine

1 clove garlic, peeled and chopped

1 tablespoon tomato paste

¼ teaspoon dried oregano

Salt and pepper to taste

¼ cup water

2 pounds codfish fillets, cut into 6 portions

1 tablespoon sour cream

2 tablespoons chopped fresh parsley

1. Heat the oil in a large nonreactive saucepan, add the peppers and onion, cover, and cook for 10 minutes, stirring occasionally. Put the cooked vegetables into a food processor or blender.

2. Pour the wine into the saucepan you used for the vegetables, add the garlic, tomato paste, oregano, and salt and pepper, and simmer briskly for 1 minute. Pour the wine sauce into the food processor or blender. Pour ¼ cup water into the saucepan, swirl to incorporate juices clinging to the pan, and add to the processor or blender. Pulse to coarsely chop the vegetables. Do not overprocess to a purée.

3. Rinse out the saucepan and place the cod pieces in it. Cover fish with cold water and season lightly with salt and pepper. Bring the water to a simmer, cover, and poach slowly for 7 to 10 minutes, or until fish flakes easily. Lift the poached fish from the pan and discard the water. Remove any bones from the fish.

4. Spoon the red pepper sauce into a saucepan and stir in the sour cream. Heat gently, but do not boil. Add the fish pieces to the sauce, spoon some sauce over them, cover, and heat for a minute or two.

5. Spoon about ¼ cup of sauce into the center of each serving dish, then a piece of cod, and top with another spoonful of sauce. Sprinkle the fish with a little chopped parsley and circle with cooked corn kernels. Pass the remaining sauce separately.

Serves 6.

Baked Herb Catfish

The sweetness of the catfish is the perfect foil for the Parmesan cheese and parsley in this dish. If possible, use the large flat-leaf variety, called Italian parsley.

Spaghetti squash, with its fluffy appearance, looks nice on the plate next to the catfish. Moisten the squash with a little warm orange juice, for an unusual flavor.

PREPARATION TIME   6 minutes
BAKING   15 minutes

4 catfish or perch fillets (about 1 pound)
½ cup grated fresh Parmesan cheese

½ cup chopped fresh parsley, preferably Italian
Pepper
2 teaspoons oil

1. Preheat oven to 375°F. If the catfish fillets are large, cut them in half lengthwise. (Each serving should be 3 to 4 ounces.) Rinse the fish and pat dry.
2. Mix the cheese, parsley, and pepper in a small bowl. Oil a baking dish that will hold the fillets comfortably. Place the fillets in the dish, skin side (darker side) down, and divide the cheese mixture among them, sprinkling it over the top.
3. Bake for about 15 minutes, or until the catfish flakes easily. (Perch fillets will take about 10 minutes.) Serve at once.

Serves 4.

HINT   Keep a piece of tightly wrapped Parmesan cheese in the freezer and as you need it cut off pieces to grate or grind. The cheese does not freeze rock solid and breaks quite easily. A mini-electric grinder reduces the cheese to crumbs in no time at all.

Baked Salmon with Vegetable Salsa

The cooking technique used in this recipe ensures the retention of all the juices in the salmon steaks. The searing seals in the moisture, then the oven heat penetrates the flesh slowly and evenly. The seared steaks should *not* be transferred to a baking dish, since the heat retained by the skillet continues the cooking process. Also, if you use a food processor, don't process all the vegetables together, since their textures vary and require different chopping times. You can, of course, chop the vegetables by hand.

Serve with steamed spinach and toasted rye croutons.

PREPARATION TIME 8 minutes

COOKING about 15 minutes

½ red pepper, cut into pieces
½ green pepper, cut into pieces
1 scallion, cut into 3 pieces
One 3-inch piece seedless
  cucumber, peeled and cut into
  pieces, or one 5-inch piece
  regular cucumber, peeled,
  seeded, and cut into pieces

1 tomato, peeled, seeded, and cut
  into chunks (page 34)
¼ cup extra-virgin olive oil
Salt and pepper
Four 5-ounce salmon steaks, each
  about ½-inch thick
1 teaspoon oil

1. Preheat oven to 200°F. Put the red and green pepper pieces in the food processor and pulse until chopped small. Do not purée. Put the peppers into a 4-cup mixing bowl.
2. Process together the cucumber, scallion, and tomato and add to the peppers in the bowl. Add the olive oil, stir, and season with a little salt and pepper. Put the salsa aside; there should be about 2 cups.
3. Season both sides of the salmon steaks with salt and pepper. Oil a nonstick ovenproof skillet and heat it until very hot. Add the salmon and sear it for about 30 seconds. Turn it over, and sear the other side for 30 seconds.
4. Immediately transfer the skillet to the oven and bake for 10 to 15 minutes, depending on the thickness of the fish. Half-inch-thick steaks should be done in 10 minutes.

5. Place salmon steaks on a warm serving dish, and top each with 2
   tablespoons of the salsa. Pass the remaining salsa in a bowl.

Serves 4.

HINT   Croutons are a tasty addition to many salads, soups, and main
course dishes. Simply cut bread into tiny squares and bake in a 375°F.
oven for about 10 minutes, or until crisp.

Salmon with Fennel Sauce

The attractive appearance and the fragrant taste of this dish belies its ease of preparation. The fennel sauce can be prepared the day before and refrigerated.

Serve with couscous or brown rice—either grain is a nice contrast to the pungency of the sauce.

PREPARATION TIME   6 minutes

COOKING   30 minutes

1 fennel bulb (1 to 1¼ pounds)
3 tablespoons milk
1 tablespoon heavy cream or half-and-half
½ to 1 teaspoon orange liqueur, preferably Grand Marnier

6 salmon steaks, each 4 to 5 ounces
Oil
Salt and pepper
6 parsley sprigs (optional)

1. Remove the stalks from the fennel bulb and cut off and reserve the small feathery leaves. Slice the bulb into quarters and in a pot of boiling water cook until very tender, 15 to 20 minutes. Drain well, then place in the food processor. (If using a blender, chop parboiled fennel by hand and purée it with liquid ingredients.) Pulse processor for a few seconds to coarsely chop fennel. Scrape down the sides of the bowl, then, with the motor running, add the milk, cream, and ½ teaspoon of the orange liqueur. Taste, and add a bit more liqueur, if desired. Pour the sauce (about 2 cups) into a small pot.
2. Select one or two heavy skillets, preferably nonstick, that hold the salmon steaks snugly. Put the skillet over high heat and rub a drop of oil over its surface with a paper towel. Once the skillet is quite hot, put in the salmon and immediately reduce the heat to medium high. When the underside of the fish is golden brown, turn, season lightly with salt and pepper, reduce the heat to medium, and cover. Cook the fish for about 10 minutes, depending on its thickness. To make sure it is done, insert the tip of a small sharp knife into the flesh near the bone—it should be flaky and have a fairly uniform color. Transfer the steaks to a warm dish and remove the skin.

3. Reheat the sauce, spoon about 3 tablespoons of it into the center of warm serving dishes, then place a salmon steak on top of the sauce. Decorate the center of each steak with the reserved fennel leaves or parsley sprigs.

Serves 6.

Poached Red Snapper

The poaching of large fish, such as red snapper, salmon, or striped bass, should begin in cold or tepid court bouillon or fish broth. The liquid must be heated gradually—if the fish is immediately plunged into hot liquid, the surface flesh will be cooked before the inside is done. A gentle approach is the key to success in this particular cooking procedure.

Cucumbers in a light creamy sauce make an elegant side dish.

PREPARATION TIME   5 minutes, plus Court Bouillon
POACHING   1 hour

1 whole red snapper, cleaned
   (about 4 pounds)
Salt and pepper
1½ quarts Court Bouillon (page
   28)
2 cups dry white wine

2 tablespoons extra-virgin olive
   oil
2 tablespoons butter or margarine
2 tablespoons lemon juice
2 lemons, quartered
Parsley sprigs for garnish

1. Rinse the fish inside and out with cold running water, pat dry, and season the cavity with salt and pepper. If using a pot that does not have a rack, wrap the fish in a piece of cheesecloth that has enough material to allow you to easily lift the snapper out of the pot. If using a fish poacher, place the snapper on the rack and lower the rack into the pan.
2. Pour the Court Bouillon and the wine over the fish. If the fish is not about three-quarters covered by the liquid, add water. Slowly heat the liquid to a simmer, but *do not boil.* Cover and poach over very low heat for about 45 minutes, or until the fish flakes easily when pierced with a fork. Lift the fish on the rack, or the wrapped fish, from the pan and drain. Discard cooking liquid, or strain, freeze, and use later in sauces.
3. While the fish is poaching, gently heat the olive oil, butter, and lemon juice in a small pot.
4. Place the fish on a platter and cut out the fins. Slit the skin from head to tail along the back and the belly, then pull the skin from the top side of the snapper. Cut down the center of the fish just to the depth of the

backbone. Then, with a long flexible knife, loosen this portion of meat from the bones, but leave it in place. Repeat with the other half.

5. Garnish a platter with the lemon halves and parsley. Pass the butter in a sauce boat. When the top portion of the snapper has been served, lift out the bone and serve the remaining portion.

Serves 4 to 6.

HINT   Cucumbers are versatile vegetables, and can be used in many ways besides being chopped raw for salads. To cook cucumbers, peel and seed, then cut into small squares. Boil until tender, about 5 minutes. Season to taste and moisten with a sauce of your choice.

Red Snapper Bayonne

Tomatoes and spicy flavors characterize much of the cuisine served in the far western region of France, hard on the Spanish border. It's up to the cook how much of the jalapeño peppers to use in this dish. A side dish of green peas or string beans provides a lively color contrast.

The sauce can be prepared the day before and reheated. If it is too thick, add some water.

PREPARATION TIME 15 minutes

COOKING 22 minutes

1 tablespoon olive oil
1 medium onion, sliced (about 1 cup)
One 1-pound can Italian plum tomatoes
1 large carrot, peeled and grated (about ¾ cup)
1 or 2 teaspoons chopped jalapeño peppers (page 35)
½ cup clam juice
½ cup dry white wine
½ tablespoon chopped basil, fresh or dried

1 bay leaf
1 teaspoon balsamic vinegar
One 2-inch piece orange rind
½ teaspoon salt
Freshly ground pepper
2 cloves garlic, peeled and minced
1 pound fish fillets such as red snapper, black sea bass, pollock, or perch
¼ cup black olives, preferably Niçoise

1. Heat the olive oil in a 12- or 14-inch nonreactive skillet. Add the onion, cover, and cook for 5 minutes. Pour the juice from the canned tomatoes into the skillet, then add tomatoes, crushing them with your hands or a large spoon as you add them.
2. Stir in the carrot, peppers, clam juice, white wine, basil, bay leaf, and balsamic vinegar. Spear the orange rind on a toothpick and add to skillet. Season with the salt and pepper and bring the sauce to a simmer. Cook for 10 minutes, uncovered, stirring often. Add the garlic and cook 3 minutes. If the sauce gets too thick, cover the pot. If you prefer a thinner sauce, add ½ cup water.
3. Rinse the fish, pat dry, and add to the skillet. Spoon some of the sauce

over the fish. Cover and cook for 4 minutes over medium heat. Turn fish, spoon more sauce over the fillets, and cook another 2 to 4 minutes.

4. Remove the fillets to a dish and divide the sauce among 4 warm plates; there will be about ½ cup per serving. Place a fillet on the sauce and garnish with the olives.

Serves 4.

HINT   When garlic is simmered in liquid for a length of time, it loses its characteristic pungency and becomes almost sweet. So, if a stronger garlic flavor is desired, add the minced garlic toward the end of the cooking time.

Shark with
Grapefruit–Red Pepper Sauce

This assertive sauce is a perfect foil for a densely textured and richly flavored fish, such as shark or swordfish. This dish is equally delicious when served cold—perfect for a warm summer evening.

To enjoy the sauce, serve a pasta with this dish. Pick an interesting shape: potpie squares, oval orzo, egg flakes, small shells, or little butterflies (farfalle).

PREPARATION TIME   12 minutes
SOAKING   (for shark) 3 hours
COOKING   10 minutes

*1½ pounds mako shark or swordfish
    steak, about 1 inch thick
2 to 3 cups low-fat or skim milk
1 whole grapefruit
1 tablespoon oil
Salt and pepper*

*1 tablespoon chopped fresh dill or
    ½ tablespoon dried
1 tablespoon butter or margarine
½ red pepper, julienned (about 1
    cup) (page 35)
1 tablespoon dry sherry*

1. If using shark, soak it first in milk. Place in a bowl or dish that will hold it snugly, and pour the milk over it. Soak for at least 3 hours, or overnight in the refrigerator.
2. Segment the grapefruit. Use a sharp, stainless steel knife and cut off both ends. Stand up the grapefruit and, using vertical strokes, cut away the skin and the white pith beneath it. To separate the segments from the membranes, hold the fruit over a bowl and slice down to the core on either side of each segment. Let the segments fall into the bowl, then lift them out of the bowl with a skimmer, remove any seeds, and reserve. Squeeze the juice from the membranes and core into the bowl; there should be about ½ cup.
3. Remove the shark from the milk, rinse, and pat dry. Smear both sides of the fish with ½ tablespoon of the oil, sprinkle with salt and pepper and ½ tablespoon dill. Place in a steamer. Turn heat on medium high and begin steaming the fish. Check fish for doneness after 7 or 8 minutes. Shark tends to cook quickly; other fish will need about 10 minutes.

4. While the fish is steaming, make the sauce. Melt the butter or margarine with the remaining ½ tablespoon oil in a 10- or 12-inch nonreactive skillet. Add the pepper strips, cover, and cook for 5 minutes. Add the grapefruit segments, stir gently, cover, and cook for 1 minute. Pour in the grapefruit juice and sherry, plus the remaining ½ tablespoon dill. Cook, uncovered, for about 2 minutes, stirring gently. Don't worry if some of the grapefruit segments break apart.
5. Cut the fish steak into 4 or 5 pieces and place on a platter or on dinner plates. Spoon the sauce over the fish and serve at once.

Serves 4 or 5.

HINT Shark tends to have an aroma with an ammoniac edge, which is perfectly natural. Neutralize it by soaking the fish in milk.

Seafood Brochettes

Seafood and meat combinations are often given the unappetizing label "surf 'n' turf," which accurately depicts what is generally put before you. But the subtle and sophisticated matching of land and sea foods *is* possible, as proven by these excellent brochettes.

Serve with a pasta salad tossed with an Oriental sauce.

PREPARATION TIME   12 minutes

MARINATING   1 hour

BROILING OR GRILLING   7 minutes

2 to 2½ pounds scallops or cod or
   monkfish fillets, cut into 1-inch
   pieces
3 shallots, finely chopped
Salt and pepper
⅓ cup oil
¾ cup dry white wine
¼ cup brandy

5 or 6 parsley sprigs
3 slices low-salt boiled ham, cut
   ¼-inch thick
12 mushroom caps
2 tablespoons butter or margarine
1 tablespoon oil
3 lemons, halved

1. Place the fish in a flat dish and sprinkle with the shallots and salt and pepper. Pour the oil, wine, and brandy over the fish until it is barely covered by the marinade. Turn the fish over to coat all surfaces. Add the parsley sprigs, cover, and put aside at room temperature for about 1 hour. Turn the fish occasionally.
2. Preheat broiler or prepare the firebed in a grill. Cut each ham slice into 12 squares. Dry the fish pieces on a towel. Thread six 10-inch skewers, beginning with a mushroom cap (rounded side out), then alternating a fish piece and a ham square. Finish with a mushroom cap, rounded side out. Melt the butter with the oil in a small pot.
3. Place the skewers on a broiler grill pan, brush with the melted butter, and broil 2 inches from the flame for about 2 minutes. Brush with the marinade and again with the butter. Broil for another 2 minutes. The total broiling time will be between 4 and 7 minutes, depending on the thickness of the fish pieces; do not overcook. Alternatively, brush the brochettes with the butter and grill over hot coals. For grilled

brochettes, serve with a sauce made by boiling the remaining marinade until reduced by one-third. If juices collect in the broiling pan, spoon over the cooked brochettes.

4. Place the grilled brochettes on heated plates and garnish with the lemon halves.

Serves 6.

HINT   Many bland foods can benefit from a light Oriental touch. Mix a few drops of dark sesame oil with corn oil, add a bit of low-sodium soy sauce, and you have an interesting sauce guaranteed to perk up any dish.

Swordfish en Escabèche

(SWORDFISH IN LEMON ASPIC)

Like most aspic dishes, this *escabèche* is best prepared a day or two ahead, which allows the flavors to mature and mellow. Although this piquant dish is especially well suited to summer dining, you can also serve it throughout the year. The *escabèche* looks most attractive when molded in a deep, round bowl, but an oblong dish makes cutting and serving easier.

PREPARATION TIME   30 minutes

COOKING   40 minutes

CHILLING AND MATURING   24 hours

¼ cup olive oil	1½ pounds swordfish, preferably
2 onions, thinly sliced	in 1 piece
4 large carrots, thinly sliced	½ cup dry vermouth
2 green peppers, thinly sliced	A few drops hot red pepper sauce
2 red peppers, thinly sliced	1 teaspoon wine vinegar
6 to 8 cloves garlic, peeled and	3 cups Fish Stock (page 27) or
sliced	clam juice
3 lemons, thinly sliced and seeded	2½ tablespoons unflavored gelatin
Salt and pepper	Chopped fresh parsley leaves

1. Heat the oil in a deep 4- or 5-quart ovenproof nonreactive casserole, and add the onions, carrots, green and red peppers, garlic, and 2 of the sliced lemons. Cover and cook very slowly for about 20 minutes, or until the vegetables are limp, but not browned. Sprinkle a little salt and pepper on the vegetables.
2. Preheat oven to 325°F. With a slotted spoon, remove half the vegetables and reserve. Spread the remaining vegetables evenly in the bottom of the pot. Place the swordfish on the vegetable bed and make a layer of the uncooked lemon slices over the fish. Cover the fish with the reserved vegetables, and pat smooth.
3. In a small bowl, mix the vermouth, hot pepper sauce, and vinegar and pour into the casserole over the fish. Pour in enough Fish Stock to almost completely cover the ingredients in the casserole. (Use as much liquid as possible so there will be a sufficient amount of aspic.)

4. Heat the liquid to a slow simmer on the stove, then place a piece of aluminum foil directly over the contents of the casserole and cover with a lid. Bake for 20 to 25 minutes, or until the swordfish begins to flake. Do not overcook. If you find the fish is slightly undercooked, let it remain in the hot liquid for a few more minutes to continue cooking.

5. Transfer the swordfish and vegetables to a colander suspended over a bowl. Drain, and reserve liquid. Cover, cool, and chill. Mix the gelatin with ¾ cup cold water and put aside for a minute or so. Reheat the cooking liquid, stir in the softened gelatin, and stir until dissolved. *Do not boil.* Remove from heat and cool. Taste for seasonings and correct if necessary. (You may want to add a little extra hot pepper sauce and vinegar.) Chill until mixture reaches a syrupy consistency.

6. Select a rectangular dish approximately 10 × 6 × 2 inches. Reserve about half the carrot slices and red pepper strips. Flake the fish into large pieces and mix with the remaining vegetables. Place in the dish. Pour on most of the syrupy aspic (reserve ½ cup) and chill until firm. Arrange the reserved carrot and red pepper slices in an attractive pattern on top and carefully spoon on the remaining aspic. Chill.

7. To serve, sprinkle with parsley and cut into squares.

Serves 10.

HINT Do not let gelatin boil or it will lose its gelling ability. Hot liquid is sufficient to dissolve the softened granules. Stir until the gelatin is completely dissolved—this will prevent the gelatin granules from sinking to the bottom of the pot and sticking.

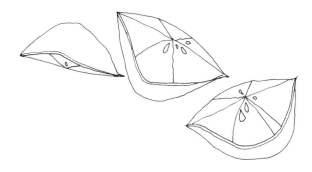

Sea Trout Plus Stuffing

In this dish, the stuffing mixture is placed *under* the fish, not in it. A tossed mixed salad that includes several raw vegetables is all you need to complete the meal.

PREPARATION TIME   10 minutes
SAUCE COOKING   10 minutes
BAKING   about 20 to 25 minutes

1 tablespoon olive oil
½ cup chopped onion
¼ pound mushrooms, sliced
¾ cup Tomato Sauce (page 31) or
  canned sauce
¾ cup white wine
½ teaspoon tarragon, fresh or
  dried

Salt and pepper
3 cups whole wheat bread cubes
  (4 or 5 slices)
A 2½-pound whole sea trout or
  bass
½ lemon, thinly sliced
1 teaspoon oil

1. Preheat oven to 425°F. Heat the oil in a 6-cup saucepan, add the onion, cover, and cook for 5 minutes. Add the mushrooms and cook, covered, 2 minutes. Pour in the Tomato Sauce and wine and season with the tarragon and salt and pepper. Cover and simmer the sauce 3 minutes.
2. Spread the bread cubes in a 14-inch gratin or baking dish. Pour the sauce over the bread and stir to mix the "stuffing."
3. Season the trout cavity with salt and pepper and fill with the lemon slices. Spread ½ teaspoon of oil on each side of the fish and place on top of the stuffing. Cover and bake for 20 to 25 minutes, or until the flesh flakes when pierced with a skewer or sharp knife.
4. Transfer the fish to a cutting board or platter and fillet it. On each dinner plate place some of the fish and the stuffing mixture.

Serves 3 or 4, depending on size of fish.

Friture d'Eperlans

(FRIED SMELTS)

The root of the word *eperlan* is *perle*, which accurately describes the pearly shine of these tiny, succulent creatures. Smelts are freshwater fish found, for the most part, in northern lakes. The supply is almost constant, except during severe winters when the lakes freeze over.

This recipe is one of the few deep-frying recipes in this book. It is included because smelts are inexpensive fish and because, cooked in this manner, they are a delicious once-in-a-while treat.

Follow this special dish with a hearty salad.

PREPARATION TIME   7 minutes
STANDING   15 minutes
COOKING   6 minutes

1½ pounds smelts, cleaned and
gutted (page 14)
1½ cups flour

Salt and pepper
Oil for deep frying
2 lemons, halved

1. Rinse the smelts and roll them in a towel to dry. Spread them on a large plate or piece of wax paper and sprinkle with salt and pepper. Pour about ¾ cup of flour onto the fish, and using both hands, toss the fish with the flour, coating them thoroughly. Let stand for about 15 minutes.
2. Meanwhile, in a deep fryer or a deep, wide skillet heat at least 3 inches of oil to 375°F. Just before frying, pour more flour on the smelts. (This second flour coating is very important, since the previously applied flour will have become damp and sticky. The second coating will cling to the first and provide a completely dry surface for crispy frying.)
3. Take a handful of smelts, shake off the excess flour, and plunge them into the hot oil, scattering them throughout the pan with a long fork or skimmer. Do not overcrowd, or you will sharply reduce the heat of the oil and prevent the coating from becoming crisp. *Fast hot frying is needed to seal the surface and prevent the absorption of fat into the fish.* The smelts will turn a dark golden color in just a few minutes.

4. Remove smelts with a skimmer and place on a baking dish lined with paper towels; keep warm in a slow oven while continuing to fry the remaining fish.

5. Sprinkle the smelts with salt and heap them onto a hot serving platter. Serve with lemon halves. You can use tartar sauce with this dish, but the smelts have such a sweet, delicate flavor that they taste better without it.

Serves 4.

Deviled Blowfish

This ugly fish has many unattractive names, blowfish, swellfish, puffer—and a few that are more appetizing, such as sea squab and chicken of the sea. Because only the back, meaty portion is eaten, the cooked fish does indeed resemble a small chicken drumstick. These spicy fish "drumsticks" are delicious cold and make an unusual addition to picnic fare.

The blowfish can marinate in the sauce for 2 to 3 hours. Once coated with the bread crumbs, fry within the hour.

Creamy scalloped potatoes made with low-fat milk is a nice balance to the spicy blowfish. Round out the meal with a serving of cole slaw.

PREPARATION TIME   11 minutes

MARINATING   15 to 30 minutes

FRYING   5 minutes

1½ pounds blowfish
2 tablespoons "hot" prepared
  mustard
3 tablespoons oil
3 tablespoons dry sherry

¼ teaspoon dried oregano
About ¾ cup bread crumbs
Oil for frying
Lemon wedges

1. With a small knife, cut off any tiny fins remaining on the fish; rinse fish and pat dry.
2. Select a shallow baking dish large enough to hold all the blowfish in a single layer. Put the mustard, oil, sherry, and oregano into the dish and stir. Add the fish pieces and turn them in the sauce until thoroughly coated with the marinade. Put aside to marinate at least 15 minutes, or longer.
3. Pour about one-fourth of the crumbs onto a large flat dish or a piece of wax paper. One by one, dip all sides of the fish in the crumbs, making sure that all surfaces are coated. Add more crumbs as needed. Put the breaded fish aside on a fresh piece of wax paper.
4. Pour oil into a 10- or 12-inch skillet to a depth of no more than ¼ inch and heat until hot. Fry the blowfish without crowding. When the first

side is nicely browned, in about 1 minute or so, turn over and cook the second side. Remove the fried fish to a warm dish and continue with the remaining fish, adding a little more oil, if necessary. Serve immediately with the lemon wedges.

Serves 4 to 6.

Smoked Haddock-Stuffed Potatoes

The emphatic flavor of the smoked haddock balances the blandness of the potato in this interesting main dish recipe. To better appreciate the unusual character of these stuffed potatoes, serve them alone as a main course, then follow with a small vegetable stew. These tasty bundles can also be served as a first course, using only a half-potato for each serving. Baked and cooled to room temperature, or even slightly chilled, they also make an unusual luncheon dish.

The potatoes can be completely prepared and stuffed ahead of time — simply cover them with plastic wrap and refrigerate for several hours. If removed from refrigerator just before baking, cook them for an extra 5 to 7 minutes.

PREPARATION TIME   35 minutes
COOKING   1¼ hours

4 baking potatoes	2 scallions, sliced
½ onion, sliced	½ teaspoon ground cumin
¾ pound smoked haddock	A few drops hot red pepper
2 to 2½ cups low-fat milk	sauce
Freshly ground pepper	⅓ cup peeled, seeded, and chopped
1 tablespoon oil	tomato (page 34)
1 tablespoon butter or margarine .	Paprika
1½ tablespoons flour	12 parsley sprigs

1. Preheat oven to 450°F. Scrub the potatoes, pierce a few times with a fork, and bake until tender, about 1 hour. Reduce oven to 350°F.
2. Select a nonreactive pot that will snugly hold the piece of smoked haddock (make sure there is at least 3 inches of space on top to avoid any spillover from the simmering milk). Make a layer of half the onion, place the fish on top, then cover with the remaining onion. Pour in the milk to almost cover the fish. Season with a generous grinding of pepper, cover the pot, and put it over low heat. Once the milk comes to a simmer, reduce the heat further and poach the haddock very slowly for 30 minutes, spooning the milk over it

occasionally. At the end of 30 minutes, lift the haddock out of the pot with a skimmer and strain and reserve the milk.

3. In a small saucepot, heat the oil and butter together, add the scallions, cover, and cook slowly for 2 minutes. Stir in the flour and whisk for a minute or two. Measure 1 cup of the poaching milk and slowly whisk it into the pot. Season with the cumin, pepper, and hot pepper sauce and simmer for 5 minutes, stirring often.

4. Remove any bones and tough outer skin from the poached haddock, and flake into small pieces. Cut the potatoes in half lengthwise and use a sturdy spoon to scoop out the cooked interior of each potato into a deep bowl. Reserve the potato shells. Using a fork, mash the potatoes into fairly small pieces. (Do not remove all the texture by mashing too fine.) Stir in three-quarters of the sauce and the flaked haddock. If the mixture seems too dry, add the remaining sauce, and as much of the poaching milk as needed. Stir in the chopped tomato. (If a stronger flavor is desired, the cooked onions from the poaching milk can be chopped and added to the filling.)

5. Fill the potato shells with the haddock mixture, sprinkle with paprika, and place on a lightly oiled baking sheet. Reheat for about 15 minutes, or until a metal skewer plunged into the center comes out almost hot.

6. Place 2 of the stuffed potatoes on each dish and tuck a small bouquet of parsley between them.

Serves 4.

HINT Parsley will keep for a week or more in the refrigerator if placed in a jar of water that is deep enough to cover the stems. Put a loose-fitting plastic bag over the top and refrigerate.

The Ultimate Crab Cakes

These special crab cakes let you taste the sweet, rich crabmeat, unadulterated by distracting bits of green and red peppers, onions, celery, and all sorts of starchy fillers. The purity of these crab cakes does make them expensive, so save them for those occasions when you want to serve something special.

Keeping the all-American character of this dish, serve with a corn pudding.

PREPARATION TIME 25 minutes

CHILLING 1¼ hours

COOKING 10 minutes

1 pound backfin crabmeat
½ cup mayonnaise
1 tablespoon prepared mustard
1 egg, beaten
Juice of 1 lemon
A few drops hot red pepper sauce
2 tablespoons chopped fresh
   parsley

1 tablespoon snipped fresh chives
½ teaspoon salt
¼ teaspoon pepper
About 1 cup bread crumbs
Oil for frying, or a mixture of
   butter and oil
4 lemon wedges
Tartar sauce

1. Pick over the crabmeat to remove any cartilage. Put crabmeat in a mixing bowl. In another small bowl, stir the mayonnaise, mustard, egg, lemon juice, hot pepper sauce, parsley, chives, salt, and pepper until well blended.
2. Spoon the sauce over the crabmeat and mix in gently. (Your hands or a wooden spoon are the best instruments for this delicate procedure.) Chill the mixture for at least 1 hour.
3. Spread half the bread crumbs on a sheet of wax paper. Form 8 crab cakes (⅓ cup each), placing each cake on the crumbs. Sprinkle the remaining crumbs over the top of each cake and pat gently to form cakes about ½-inch thick. Add more crumbs as needed. Carefully place the cakes on a baking sheet lined with wax paper. Chill for at least 15 minutes.

4. Pour oil into a frying pan, to the depth of ¼ inch. Heat the oil and when hot, add a few crab cakes. Do not crowd the pan. When the underside is brown, turn each cake carefully and brown the other side. Transfer the browned cakes to a paper towel to drain, then to a warm dish.
5. Let the crab cakes stand for at least 5 minutes. (Their flavor is best when warm, not hot.) Garnish with the lemon wedges and serve with the tartar sauce.

Serves 4.

HINT   Fresh chives are delicate; they crush easily when chopped with a knife. Snip them with scissors, instead.

Bluefish Cakes

The stronger, richer taste of the inexpensive bluefish acts as a good substitute for the delicate flavor of crabmeat in these excellent cakes. You can use leftover bluefish that has been baked, steamed, or poached. However, these patties are so good, you won't mind the extra step of steaming the fish just to make them (page 24).

A good partner to this dish is peas mixed with sautéed scallions.

PREPARATION TIME 35 minutes
CHILLING 1¼ hours
COOKING 10 minutes

1 pound bluefish, cooked
½ cup fresh or frozen corn
   kernels, cooked
2 tablespoons chopped pimiento
1¼ cups plain bread crumbs
2 scallions, chopped
¼ cup chopped fresh parsley
½ cup mayonnaise

1 tablespoon prepared mustard
2 tablespoons lemon juice
½ teaspoon light soy sauce
A few drops hot red pepper sauce
Salt and pepper
Oil for frying
4 lemon wedges
Tartar sauce

1. Flake the cooked bluefish into a mixing bowl. Add the corn, pimiento, ¼ cup of the bread crumbs, scallions, and parsley. Mix well.
2. In a small bowl, stir the mayonnaise, mustard, lemon juice, soy sauce, hot pepper sauce, salt, and pepper and pour over the fish mixture. Mix well to blend. Chill for at least 1 hour.
3. Spread half the bread crumbs on a sheet of wax paper. Form 8 bluefish cakes (⅓ cup each), and place each cake on the crumbs. Sprinkle the remaining crumbs over the top of each cake and pat gently to form cakes about ½-inch thick. Add more bread crumbs as needed. Carefully place the cakes on a baking sheet lined with wax paper. Chill at least 15 minutes.
4. Pour oil into a frying pan to a depth of ¼ inch. Heat the oil and when hot add a few fish cakes. Do not crowd the pan. When the underside is brown, turn carefully and brown the other side. Drain cakes on paper towel and keep warm.

5. Let the bluefish cakes stand for at least 5 minutes. Garnish with the lemon wedges and serve with the tartar sauce.

Serves 4.

Moules à la Marinère

(STEAMED MUSSELS)

This classic dish has become a great favorite. It's ideal for a light summer meal. Serve with a salad and lots of crusty bread to soak up the sauce.

PREPARATION TIME 20 minutes

COOKING 20 minutes

2 cups water
1 large onion, finely chopped
Large herb bouquet (8 parsley
  sprigs, 1 large bay leaf, tops of
  2 celery ribs, bundled and tied
  together with kitchen twine)
1 tablespoon juniper berries
  (optional, but recommended)

½ teaspoon dried thyme
½ teaspoon salt
¼ teaspoon pepper
1 carrot, finely diced
½ lemon
5 pounds mussels
1½ cups dry white wine

1. In a large pot, combine the water, onion, herb bouquet, juniper berries, thyme, salt, pepper, and carrot. Squeeze the juice of the lemon into the water, and add the lemon half as well. Cover, bring to a boil, and simmer for 15 minutes. (This can be done in advance and the pot put aside for the final few minutes of cooking.)
2. Scrub and clean the mussels following the directions on page 17.
3. Pour the white wine into the simmering broth and bring it back to a full boil. Add the mussels and cover tightly. Cook at a high heat and shake the pot once or twice during the cooking to move the mussels around, or stir the mussels quickly with a large spoon. The mussels should open in no more than 5 minutes. Discard any that have not opened.
4. Ladle the mussels into deep soup bowls and strain the broth over them. Do not use all of the cooking broth, since there will be grit at the bottom. Provide a big bowl in the center of the table for the shells.

Serves 4 to 6.

HINT Use a complete mussel shell, in a pincerlike fashion, to pluck out the morsels of meat in the other shells.

Shrimp and Vegetable Stir-Fry

This dish makes an impressive presentation. If you prefer, you can serve it with rice instead of the noodles.

PREPARATION TIME   15 minutes
COOKING   6 minutes

6 cups water
2 ounces cellophane noodles
2 tablespoons oil
2 cloves garlic, peeled and
  smashed (page 36)
3 slices fresh ginger
½ pound medium shrimp, peeled
  and deveined
4 scallions, cut into 2-inch
  lengths
½ red pepper, sliced

1 small turnip (about 4 ounces),
  peeled and cut into matchstick
  lengths (page 35)
¼ pound mushrooms, sliced
1 tablespoon cornstarch
1¼ cups Chicken Stock (page 29)
1 tablespoon light soy sauce
¼ pound spinach, washed and
  torn into pieces
1 tablespoon dry sherry
½ teaspoon dark sesame seed oil

1. While preparing the vegetables, bring the water to a boil. Put the noodles in a deep bowl, pour the boiling water over them, cover, and put aside for 15 minutes. Drain well.
2. In a wok or a heavy 12-inch skillet, warm the oil over medium heat. Add the garlic and ginger and cook until they turn brown, pressing the browned pieces to release as much of their oils as possible. (If time permits, do this in advance, cover, and let the flavorings steep in the oil. When ready to proceed, remove the garlic and ginger with a skimmer and discard.)
3. Heat the oil until hot, add the shrimp, and cook them very quickly, constantly turning them over, for 30 seconds or so. With the skimmer remove the shrimp to a bowl.
4. Put the scallions in the wok or skillet and cook for 30 seconds, stirring all the while. Add the red pepper and turnips, stir, cover, and cook for 2 minutes. Add the mushrooms and stir-fry for 1 minute. Mix ¼ cup of the Chicken Stock with the cornstarch, stir, and reserve. Pour the

remaining 1 cup stock and the soy sauce into the wok or skillet and cook for 30 seconds, stirring the vegetables.

5. Add the cornstarch mixture to the vegetables and simmer for 30 seconds. Return the shrimp to the skillet, add the spinach, and cook for a few seconds. Remove the pan from the heat and stir in the sherry and sesame seed oil.

6. Make a bed of the softened noodles on a warm serving dish and top with the shrimp-vegetable mixture.

Serves 4.

Stir-Fried Shrimp and Mahimahi

The contrast between the two fish textures, shapes, and colors adds extra interest to this quick and easy dish. Boiled white or brown rice is the traditional accompaniment.

The flavored oil can be made well ahead of time, and all of the fish, shrimp, and vegetables can be prepared in advance, covered, and refrigerated.

PREPARATION TIME 20 minutes

COOKING 10 minutes

3 tablespoons oil
3 cloves garlic, peeled and sliced
6 slices fresh ginger
½ pound medium shrimp, peeled
   and deveined
½ pound fish steak such as
   mahimahi, shark, or marlin
2 teaspoons cornstarch

2 tablespoons dry sherry
1 tablespoon light soy sauce
½ red pepper, cut into strips
6 scallions, cut into 1-inch lengths
2 cups peas, cooked if fresh,
   thoroughly defrosted if frozen
1 cup clam juice
½ teaspoon dark sesame seed oil

1. Pour the oil into a wok or large round-bottomed skillet. Add the garlic and ginger, place over low heat, cover, and cook for about 5 minutes, or until the garlic and ginger have turned a dark golden brown. Let the flavorings steep in the oil.

2. Meanwhile, cut the shrimp in half crosswise. Cut the fish steak into 1-inch strips and combine with the shrimp in a bowl. In a small bowl, stir the cornstarch, sherry, and soy sauce, then pour over the fish. Mix well to coat all surfaces of the fish.

3. Remove the garlic and ginger from the oil in the wok with a skimmer. Heat the oil until medium hot, add the red pepper and scallions, cover, and cook for about 3 minutes. Increase the heat to high, add the shrimp and fish steak with their seasonings, and cook quickly, constantly turning each piece over with a spatula. Cook until the fish firms and the shrimp begin to turn pink.

4. Add the peas and clam juice, cover, and cook for about 30 seconds, just long enough to heat the peas and thicken the sauce. Add the sesame seed oil, cover, turn off the heat, and let the mixture stand for 1 minute. Serve at once.

Serves 4.

Scampi Fritti

(BATTER-FRIED SHRIMP)

Traditionally, these succulent shrimp are served alone. Follow them with warm asparagus dressed with vinaigrette and sprinkled with lots of chopped fresh herbs.

PREPARATION TIME   20 minutes

MARINATING   30 minutes

FRYING   about 5 minutes

1 pound medium or large shrimp, peeled and deveined, tails left intact

½ cup dry white wine

1 shallot, minced

2 tablespoons extra-virgin olive oil

Salt and pepper

Batter

2 cups flour

1 teaspoon salt

1½ tablespoons baking powder

1½ cups ice water

Oil for frying

3 lemons, halved

Tartar sauce or mayonnaise mixed with a little Pesto (page 32) (optional)

1. In a large bowl, mix the shrimp, wine, shallot, and olive oil, and lightly season with salt and pepper. Mix well to coat all shrimp surfaces with the marinade. Put aside for about 30 minutes.
2. Prepare the batter just before you intend to use it to maintain its cold temperature. In a bowl, whisk the flour, salt, and baking powder, then slowly add 1 cup of the ice water. Whisk until very smooth. Add additional ice water until the batter reaches the consistency of heavy cream. Do not make the batter too thin.
3. Select 1 or 2 skillets for frying the shrimp and pour in oil to a depth of about ½ inch. Heat until quite hot. Lift the shrimp, 1 at a time, by the tail and dip into the batter. Drop the batter-coated shrimp into the hot oil. Do not crowd the skillet(s) because the batter will puff up. After about 30 seconds, turn the shrimp and fry the other sides. When

golden brown on both sides, lift the shrimp with a skimmer and transfer to a heated plate lined with paper towels. Keep warm while frying the remaining shrimp.

4. Mound the shrimp in the center of a warm serving dish and surround with the lemon halves. Pass the tartar sauce or mayonnaise, if using. Serve at once.

Serves 4.

HINT   The secret to nongreasy frying is to cook *quickly*. While oil bubbles are still shooting out from the batter, no grease is being absorbed. When the bubbles diminish, grease begins to penetrate the batter.

Savoy Cabbage Shrimp Rolls

The humble cabbage turns glamorous in this unusual treatment. The Savoy cabbage not only has a subtle flavor, it also has nicely crimped leaves that add a lacy pattern to the cooked rolls.

This dish would make a modestly priced and convenient main course for a dinner party—the rolls can be completely prepared the day before, refrigerated, and steamed just before serving. A food processor is needed to make this dish.

Serve it with a carrot purée sparked with a little cooked pear.

PREPARATION TIME 40 minutes

CHILLING 30 minutes

COOKING 50 minutes

1 small head Savoy cabbage
  (about 2 pounds)
½ cup dry white wine
One 2-inch piece celery
¼ lemon
Salt and pepper
½ pound medium shrimp
1 shallot, chopped
1 teaspoon anchovy paste

1 slice soft white bread
½ cup milk
1 tomato, peeled, seeded, and
  chopped (page 34)
½ pound sole or flounder fillets
Hot red pepper sauce
1 egg white
¼ cup light cream
1 cup Chive Sauce (page 33)

1. Cut the core from the cabbage. Discard the thick, outer leaves. Carefully cut off 14 leaves, put them into a deep pot, and pour 1 cup cold water over them. Bring water to a boil, turn down heat, cover, and steam leaves until soft and pliable, about 20 minutes. To cool, pour cold water into pot. When leaves can be handled, drain off water and pat them dry. Trim off thick base of each with a paring knife. Chill leaves.

2. To make the puréed filling, in a saucepan, boil ¼ cup of the wine, ¾ cup water, and the celery, covered, for about 5 minutes. Squeeze the juice from the lemon wedge into the pan, toss in the lemon wedge, and add salt and pepper. Add one-quarter of the shrimp, cover, reduce

143

heat, and cook for 1 minute. Drain the shrimp and cool. Discard liquid. Peel, devein, and mince shrimp. Chill.

3. In a small pot, boil the shallot with the remaining ¼ cup of the wine until reduced by half. Add the anchovy paste and stir to dissolve. Cool, then chill. Cut off and discard crusts from the bread, tear the slice into small pieces, then soak in ¼ cup of milk for 5 minutes. Squeeze out as much milk from bread as possible, then place bread in a food processor.

4. Put the tomato pieces in a small sieve to drain. Peel and devein the remaining uncooked shrimp and cut in half. Cut the fish fillets into 1-inch chunks. Add the raw shrimp, fish chunks, and tomato to the food processor and season with the hot pepper sauce and salt and pepper. Pulse machine just to combine. Scrape down the sides. With motor running, add the egg white and the remaining ¼ cup milk. Scrape down the sides again, and pour in the cream. If you wish to adjust seasonings, poach a teaspoon of the filling in simmering water. Taste and correct seasoning, if necessary. Fold the chilled shrimp into the filling. Refrigerate for 30 minutes.

5. Spread out cabbage leaves. Divide the shrimp filling among 10 leaves, folding in the sides of each after first rolling it up. (Use extra cooked leaves to patch where necessary.) Put the finished rolls on a rack in a steamer, seam side down. Pour boiling water into the steamer, making sure the water does not touch the rack. Cover, bring to a boil, reduce heat, and simmer until the rolls feel firm to the touch, about 20 to 25 minutes.

6. Transfer rolls to warm plates and top with the Chive Sauce.

Serves 5.

Steamed Soft-Shell Clams

Few shellfish require as little preparation as clams. A quick scrub under running water is all you need to do; a few minutes in the pot and you have one of America's great classic dishes.

Use soft-shell clams, also known as longnecks, for this dish. They are cheaper than hard-shell clams, are tender and sweet when properly cooked, and come equipped with a little tail to accommodate easy finger eating.

Serve with corn-on-the-cob and a fresh tomato salad.

PREPARATION TIME 5 minutes
COOKING 4 minutes

2½ pounds soft-shell clams (about
  4 dozen)
¼ teaspoon celery seeds

1 cup water
1 lemon, quartered

Sauce
(optional)

4 tablespoons butter
¼ cup dry white wine

1 teaspoon light soy
  sauce

1. Scrub the clams with a stiff brush under cold running water, and place them in a 6- to 8-quart pot. The clams should be shut tight; discard any that remain open after you tap them. Sprinkle celery seeds on the clams, and pour in the water. Place the pot over high heat, and as soon as the water comes to a boil, cover, and steam for about 4 or 5 minutes, or just until the shells open. Shake the pot once or twice during the cooking to turn the clams over and distribute them more evenly over the heat.
2. While the clams are cooking, prepare the butter sauce, if using. Melt the butter with the wine and soy sauce. For each diner, you will need a deep bowl for the clams, a cup and saucer for the broth, and a small custard cup and saucer for the butter sauce. Place a large bowl for shells in the center of the table.
3. With a skimmer, lift the clams out of the pot, and divide them among

the bowls, discarding any that have not opened. Pour the clam broth from the pot into a warmed pitcher, leaving behind any sand that has collected on the bottom. Pour the optional butter sauce into the small cups. Last, pour the clam broth into their cups, again leaving behind any sand at the bottom of the pitcher.

4. Serve clams. To eat: pull off the shells and remove the dark neck skin that covers the siphon (neck) and discard. Hold the clam by the siphon, dip it into the clam broth, and eat. If you like, you can also treat each clam to a few drops of lemon juice or a quick dip in the butter sauce. The broth also makes a delicious drink. Provide plenty of paper napkins.

Serves 4.

HINT   Leftover clam cooking broth can be strained (preferably through a double layer of cheesecloth or a dish towel), decanted into small containers, and frozen for future use in fish soups and stews.

Sautéed Soft-Shell Crabs

Fresh soft-shell crabs are one of the glories of the American spring and early summer. The East Coast is especially favored by their availability. If there is a fisherman in your house who is lucky enough to bring in a catch of soft shells, and you want to freeze them, do not clean them first, since much of their juice will be lost in the cleaning. Actually, soft shells are much better eaten fresh in season; freezing does not help their texture or taste.

This recipe is the classic way to cook soft shells—they retain their crispness with just a little sauce to enhance the flavor.

Corn kernels with chopped pimiento make a colorful addition to this dish.

PREPARATION TIME   10 minutes
COOKING   6 minutes

12 large or 18 medium soft-shell crabs	Salt and pepper
	Juice of 1 lemon
4 tablespoons butter or margarine	¾ to 1 cup dry white wine
¼ cup oil	½ cup chopped fresh parsley
½ to ¾ cup flour	3 lemons, halved

1. Rinse the crabs under cold running water, shake off the excess water, and place the crabs between paper towels.
2. It is best to use 2 skillets because the crabs must sauté in 1 layer. Melt 1 tablespoon of the butter or margarine and add 1 tablespoon of the oil to each skillet. Spread the flour on a sheet of wax paper and lightly coat each crab on both sides; shake off the excess. (If the flouring is done in advance, the coating will become damp and prevent browning.) Place the crabs in the hot pans. Cover.
3. After about 1 minute, sprinkle the crabs with salt and pepper, cover, and sauté for 2 minutes more.
4. Turn the crabs, adding more butter and oil as necessary. Sprinkle again with salt and pepper and squeeze the juice of a lemon over them. Cover and sauté for 1 minute.

5. Pour in the wine and baste the crabs with some of the sauce. Cover and sauté for 2 minutes more, basting once or twice. When done, the crabs should be a vibrant red under their golden coating.

6. Sprinkle the parsley over the crabs and cover the skillets again for a few seconds. Place 2 or 3 crabs on warmed plates and spoon some of the sauce over each. Garnish with a lemon half.

Serves 6.

Oriental Soft-Shell Crabs

Soft-shell crabs are fairly small, but their meat is rich enough to tolerate a few intense flavors. For a change of pace, try this unusual and tasty version.

Steamed rice is the traditional accompaniment to this dish.

PREPARATION TIME   12 minutes
MARINATING   15 minutes
COOKING   3 minutes

8 soft-shell crabs
2 tablespoons light soy sauce
¼ cup sweet sherry
Freshly ground black pepper
2 tablespoons oil
12 scallions, chopped
1 teaspoon finely chopped, peeled
    fresh ginger

1 clove garlic, peeled and minced
2 tablespoons fermented black
    beans,* rinsed well, drained,
    and chopped
¼ tablespoon hot red pepper
    flakes, or to taste
1 cup Chicken Stock (page 29) or
    canned broth

1. Rinse the crabs, pat dry, and place in a shallow dish. Combine the soy sauce, sherry, and pepper, and pour over the crabs. Turn the crabs over several times to thoroughly coat them with the marinade. Put aside for 15 minutes.
2. Select 2 skillets that will each hold 4 crabs. Heat 1 tablespoon oil in each. When oil is hot, lift the crabs out of the dish, shake off the excess marinade, and put into the skillets. (Reserve marinade.) Fry crabs quickly for about 30 seconds on each side, just enough to crisp the skin. Remove the crabs.
3. Make the sauce in only 1 skillet. To the remaining oil add the scallions, garlic, ginger, black beans, and pepper flakes. Stir with a wooden spoon to scrape the pan juices up into the sauce and cook for 30 seconds, stirring all the while. Add the reserved marinade and Chicken Stock, cover, and simmer another 30 seconds.
4. Discard oil in the second skillet. Return 4 crabs to the empty skillet and spoon half the sauce over them. Add the remaining 4 crabs to the

first skillet with the sauce. Cover both skillets and simmer for about 30 seconds. Turn crabs and cook for a final 30 seconds.
5. Place 2 crabs on each warm plate and spoon sauce over them. Serve at once.

Serves 4.

*Fermented black beans are available in the Oriental section of most supermarkets or specialty food stores.

Steamed Lobster

This recipe calls for a somewhat unorthodox method of cooking whole lobsters. According to a Maine fisherman, dropping lobsters into a huge pot of boiling water is unnecessary. It's better, he explained, to steam the lobster in an inch or so of water. You run no risk of burning yourself with the boiling water, and it is far easier to retrieve the cooked lobsters. Most important, the meat is more succulent and tender.

Serve with homemade potato salad.

PREPARATION TIME   2 minutes
COOKING   12 minutes

4 lobsters, each weighing between   *Water*
1 and 1¼ pounds   *Melted butter, or a combination of*
Seaweed (optional)   *half butter and half margarine*

1. Select a kettle large and deep enough to hold the lobsters, such as a soup kettle or stockpot. If the lobsters were packed with seaweed, rinse the strands and place in the bottom of the pot. Add about 1 inch of water.
2. Bring the water to a boil, quickly add the lobsters, cover, and cook them over medium heat. Allow 5 minutes for the first pound and 3 minutes for each additional pound. The color of the shell will indicate whether the meat is thoroughly cooked or not. If the shells are a vibrant orange-red, the lobsters are not ready. When the red deepens and takes on a burned orange hue, they are. Remove the lobsters with tongs, and allow them to drain for a minute or two.
3. Use small platters for the lobsters and place a large bowl for the discarded shells in the center of the table. Place a cup of hot melted butter at each place setting, along with a knife, fork, and nutcracker.

Serves 4.

Broiled Lobster

This is one of the simplest and best ways to prepare lobster. The split lobsters are painted with an unusual mustard sauce that protects and moistens the sweet meat underneath. The pungency of the mustard almost totally disappears, leaving behind a tasty succulence.

To retain as much juice as possible, the lobsters should be split just before broiling. If you prefer to have the fish store do that for you, buy them as close to cooking time as possible.

PREPARATION TIME   5 minutes
BROILING   about 10 minutes

¼ cup smooth Dijon-style mustard
2 tablespoons oil
2 tablespoons brandy

Two 1- to 1¼-pound lobsters
1 lemon, cut into wedges
(optional)

1. Combine the mustard, oil, and brandy in a small bowl. Using a whisk, mix thoroughly. Split the lobsters* and pull out and discard the stomach (a hard sand sac near the head) and the intestinal vein that runs through the middle of the underside of the tail meat.
2. Preheat broiler. Place the 4 lobster halves in a heavy baking pan, shell side up. Broil 3 minutes; using tongs, carefully turn the lobsters over, shell side down. Liberally brush with mustard sauce and broil for about 7 or 8 minutes, or until the shells are a bright burned orange.
3. Transfer the cooked lobsters to warm platters and serve at once. Provide a nutcracker and lobster pick for each person, and a lemon wedge, if desired.

Serves 2.

HINT   Some cooks like to make use of the black roe, or coral, and the greenish brown liver, or tomalley, of the lobster in stuffings and sauces. Both are considered delicacies and are prized by many for their deep sea flavor. However, others may prefer to heed our advice on the safety of consuming these parts of the shellfish (see page 3).

*To split lobsters, use a very sturdy, 12-inch knife. Steady the lobster, shell side up. Place the tip of the knife behind the center of the head. Plunge the knife through the shell and quickly split the shell in two, working toward the tail, then turn the lobster over and sever the head.

Squid with Asparagus

The cuisines of Mediterranean countries and the Orient are replete with intriguing preparations for squid. Venetian cooking is noted for squid in its own ink, a murky dish with a rich, briny flavor. In southern France squid is often stewed with fresh green olives, while in the Far East squid pieces are quickly stir-fried with various greens. International cooks take full advantage of the great economy in serving squid, which is inexpensive and a good source of protein.

This delicious dish appeals even to those who thought they didn't like squid.

PREPARATION TIME   20 minutes
COOKING   35 minutes

2 tablespoons olive oil
1 clove garlic, peeled
1 dried hot red chili, seeded
  (page 35)
2 pounds squid, cleaned and cut
  into rings (page 19)

1½ cups dry white wine
Salt and pepper
½ pound fresh asparagus
¼ cup snipped fresh chives

1. Heat the oil in a wide skillet over medium heat. Add the garlic and chili pepper and cook until brown; remove with a skimmer and discard.
2. Add the squid rings to the skillet, and, stirring often, cook for about 3 or 4 minutes, or until they are slightly firm. Pour in the wine, reduce the heat, and cook until the squid are almost tender and the wine is mostly evaporated. Reduce the heat, sprinkle with salt and pepper, cover, and simmer for about 15 minutes.
3. Meanwhile, snap off the woody stems of the asparagus and cut the green stalk and the tip into long, thin diagonal slices. When the squid are tender, add the asparagus, cover, and cook another minute or two, until the asparagus is cooked through but still crisp.
4. Divide the squid and asparagus among 6 warm plates and garnish with the chopped chives.

Serves 6.

Stuffed Squid

The smooth, triangular-shaped body of the squid is perfect for tasty stuffings. This recipe takes a bit longer to do than many in this book, but none of the steps are difficult. If you like, regular rice, which cooks faster than barley, can be substituted, but you sacrifice the extra nutty flavor and the satiny texture of the barley. Serve with steamed spinach or broccoli.

This dish tastes even better if made one or two days in advance, refrigerated, and then reheated.

PREPARATION TIME   35 minutes
COOKING   1¾ hours

6 large squid (the sac should
   measure at least 5 inches, not
   including the tentacles)

Stuffing

2 tablespoons olive oil
½ small onion, chopped (about ¼
   cup)
1 clove garlic, peeled and
   minced
½ cup pearl barley
2¼ cups water
Salt and pepper
2 scallions, chopped

¼ cup peeled red pepper (page
   34), diced, or chopped pimiento
¼ cup mushrooms, chopped
   (about 3 small)
2 tablespoons chopped fresh
   parsley
1 tablespoon chopped fresh basil
¼ cup dry white wine
Salt and pepper

Braising sauce

1 cup canned chopped plum
   tomatoes with juice
½ cup dry white wine
1 clove garlic, peeled and chopped
½ small onion, chopped

One 1-inch piece orange zest,
   speared on a toothpick
¼ teaspoon vinegar, preferably
   balsamic or red wine
A pinch saffron

1. To make stuffing: heat the oil in a heavy 4-cup pot. Add the onion, cover, and cook for about 5 minutes. Add the garlic and pearl barley and cook for another minute, stirring all the while. Pour in the water, season with salt and pepper, cover, and cook for about 45 minutes, stirring occasionally. Pour into a mixing bowl and allow to cool a few minutes.

2. While the barley is cooking, clean the squid according to the directions on page 19. Cut off the tentacles and pull off the wings, chop up both, and add to the pot of barley.

3. Complete the stuffing by adding the scallions, red pepper, mushrooms, parsley, basil, wine, and salt and pepper. Stuff the squid loosely; do not overfill. Close the opening with toothpicks.

4. Select a nonreactive skillet or casserole that will hold the stuffed squid snugly. (The squid shrinks as it cooks.) To make braising sauce: Put the tomatoes, wine, garlic, onion, orange zest, vinegar, saffron, and salt and pepper in the skillet or casserole and bring to a simmer. Cover and cook for 5 minutes.

5. Add the squid to the skillet. The heat will contract the sacs into puffy little "packages." Cover and braise for 50 minutes to 1 hour, or until a small sharp knife cuts easily into the squid. Baste occasionally during the cooking.

6. Transfer the squid to a serving platter or onto individual dishes and pull out the toothpicks. Remove and discard the orange zest and spoon some of the sauce over each serving. The squid can also be cut into thick slices. In that case let the cooked squid stand for about 5 minutes before cutting.

Serves 6.

HINT Add any leftover stuffing to the braising sauce for the last 10 minutes or so of cooking. Its addition will create a creamier sauce and increase the heartiness of the dish.

Pastas and Risottos

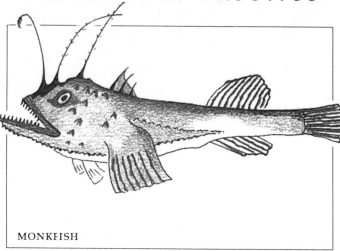

MONKFISH

Traditionally, pasta or risotto is a preliminary dish in
a multi-course meal. Today's lighter eating habits,
however, mean that both dishes are served more
often as a main course. Pasta, of course, is a fixture
on most restaurant menus as well as in our own
kitchens. Risotto, a specialty of some of our more
upscale restaurants, demands more attention during
the cooking process, and is not an everyday dish in
most American homes. But this creamy rice dish
can be enjoyed at home anytime. There is no
particular mystique about its preparation—all
you need is a little patience.
When preparing and serving pastas or risottos, it

pays to observe a few traditional rules. Do not, for instance, serve grated cheese with fish pastas or risottos. Pay careful attention to the weight and richness of the sauce, especially when combining it with a pasta. Fresh pasta should not be pitted against a heavy ragu, and a thin savory sauce does better when paired with flat linguine or the thin strands of angel hair pasta. And fresh pasta is not always preferable to the commercially dried macaroni product. Again, it's a matter of correctly matching textures, consistencies, and flavors.

Linguine with Clam Sauce

The best clam sauce is made with fresh clams, which, unfortunately, need to be shucked. This task is simple for cooks adept with a clam knife, but for others, it's a formidable undertaking. Many recipes solve the problem by suggesting canned clams, but although there are many useful and tasty canned products, clams are definitely not among them. For this reason, try using fresh soft-shell clams. They only need a brief cooking to open their shells, and they do not toughen when the sauce is reheated. Serve with warm garlic bread and a green salad.

PREPARATION TIME   13 minutes

COOKING   25 minutes

2 pounds soft-shell clams
2 tablespoons olive oil
2 cloves garlic, peeled and minced
2 cups peeled, seeded, and
   chopped tomatoes (page 34), or
   One 1-pound can whole
   tomatoes

½ teaspoon fennel seeds
Salt and pepper
½ pound linguine
½ cup chopped fresh
   parsley

1. Steam the clams, remove the shells, and discard (page 145). Carefully strain the clam cooking broth, pouring it through a double layer of cheesecloth or dish towel and discarding the sand in the bottom of the pot. Cut off the tails of the clams, reserving just the plump bodies.
2. In a heavy 4-cup nonreactive saucepan, heat the oil, add the garlic, cover, and cook for 30 seconds. Add the tomatoes; if using canned tomatoes pour in the juice, then crush the tomatoes using your hands or the back of a large spoon as you add them to the pan. Add 1 cup of clam broth, fennel seeds, and salt and pepper. Bring the sauce to a boil and simmer until reduced and quite thick, about 15 to 20 minutes.
3. Meanwhile, bring about 6 quarts of water to a boil in a large pot. Add a few drops of oil and a sprinkling of salt, if desired. Slowly add the linguine, a handful at a time, to maintain the water at a constant boil. Cook until al dente (slightly firm), about 30 seconds for fresh pasta, and 7 to 8 minutes for dried. Drain the linguine into a large colander,

shake well, then stir with a long-handled fork to eliminate any remaining water.

4. Bring the sauce to a slow simmer, add the clams and all but 2 tablespoons of the parsley, and cook briefly to warm the shellfish.

5. Divide the linguine among 4 warm plates and spoon the sauce over it. Garnish each plate with a sprinkling of fresh chopped parsley, and serve immediately.

Serves 4.

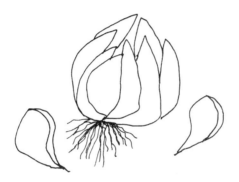

Fettuccine with Tuna Sauce

This is an excellent pasta dish in which slices of flavorful seared fresh tuna dominate the sauce. Use dried fettuccine here because its sturdier texture is more compatible with the sliced fish.

PREPARATION TIME   15 minutes
CHILLING   30 minutes
COOKING   15 minutes

¾ pound tuna steak
2 tablespoons olive oil
4 scallions, chopped
½ red pepper, chopped
½ cup peeled and chopped tomato
(page 34) or chopped, canned
whole tomatoes

1 cup dry red wine
¼ teaspoon fresh dill or ¼
teaspoon dried
Salt and pepper
1 tablespoon capers, rinsed and
drained
½ pound dried fettuccine

1. Tightly cover the tuna steak in plastic wrap and freeze for about 30 minutes. (This chilling firms the fish for slicing.) Slice into strips about ⅛-inch thick, 1 inch wide, and 3 inches long. Reserve any tuna fragments.
2. Pour 1 tablespoon of the oil into a heavy deep skillet or saucepot, heat well, then quickly sear half the tuna slices on both sides, allowing just a few seconds per side. Transfer tuna to a dish and reserve. Repeat with remaining oil and tuna.
3. Add the scallions and red pepper to the skillet, mix well, cover, and sauté over medium heat for 2 minutes. Add the tomato, wine, dill, and salt and pepper, cover, and simmer 5 minutes. Add the capers and cook the sauce another minute.
4. Meanwhile, bring water to a boil in a large 6-quart pot. Add a few drops of oil and a sprinkling of salt, if desired. Add the fettuccine, a little at a time, to maintain a rolling boil. Cover the pot to bring the water back to a boil, then uncover and cook the pasta for about 10 minutes. Drain the fettuccine into a large colander, then stir with a long-handled fork to eliminate any remaining water.
5. Add the seared tuna and the fragments to the simmering sauce. Cook for no more than 30 seconds.
6. Divide the fettuccine among 4 warm plates and spoon the sauce and tuna over the pasta. Serve immediately.

Serves 4.

Pasta with Swordfish Ragu

You need a firm-textured fish for this dish because a more delicate one would disintegrate in the sauce. The time needed to cook the fish also allows for a deeper intensity of flavor in the ragu. A shaped pasta, such as *rotini* (macaroni twists) or shells, works best in this hearty dish.

The sauce tastes even better if made the day before and refrigerated. Add the basil and garlic (Step 3) when reheating the sauce.

PREPARATION TIME   20 minutes
COOKING   30 minutes

Sauce

¼ cup olive oil
½ cup chopped onion
¼ cup chopped fresh parsley
2 medium carrots, peeled and
   chopped
¼ cup chopped fresh basil

4 cloves garlic, peeled and
   chopped
2 cups fresh Tomato Sauce (page
   31), or canned
½ cup dry red wine
1 tablespoon lemon juice

½ pound swordfish, tuna, or
   shark, cut into pieces
Salt and pepper to taste
1 pound rotini or shell-shaped
   pasta

1 tablespoon oil
3 tablespoons chopped fresh
   parsley (optional)

1. To make sauce: in a 4- or 5-cup saucepan heat the oil, then add the onion, parsley, carrots, 2 tablespoons of the basil, and half the garlic. Sauté for about 5 minutes, stirring occasionally. Add the Tomato Sauce, wine, and lemon juice and simmer, uncovered, for 5 minutes.
2. Add the fish and cook at a slow simmer for about 10 minutes. Stir the sauce occasionally, crushing the fish against the sides of the pan. As the fish breaks up it will absorb more of the sauce, which will become quite thick.
3. Taste for salt and pepper and correct, if necessary. Add the remaining 2 tablespoons basil and garlic, cover, and cook a final 5 minutes.

4. Cook the pasta in at least 5 quarts of boiling water to which the remaining oil and a little salt has been added. Cook for 7 to 9 minutes, or until just tender. Drain at once.
5. Divide the pasta among 6 warm plates, spoon the sauce over all, and garnish with the parsley, if desired. Serve at once.

Serves 6.

HINT   Here's an easy, professional way to squeeze lemon juice: Put a cut lemon half on the edge of a clean white kitchen towel, twist the cloth taut, and squeeze. The juice comes out, the seeds stay behind. Lemon juice is a great natural bleach, so the towel will be cleaner looking than before. Rinse the towel with hot water and return it to its rack.

Fettuccine with
Mahimahi-and-Pepper Sauce

The yellow and red bell peppers add a colorful note to this subtly flavored fish dish. Don't substitute the more strongly flavored green peppers; they tend to dominate the sauce.

You can prepare the sauce in advance without adding the potato starch or the fish. Flake the fish just before adding to the sauce, to retain its juiciness.

PREPARATION TIME   15 minutes
COOKING   25 minutes

1 pound mahimahi or swordfish
2 tablespoons olive oil
1 medium onion, sliced (about 1 cup)
2 cloves garlic, peeled and minced
1 cup red pepper, julienned (page 35)
1 cup yellow pepper, julienned
1/4 pound mushrooms
2 cups Fish Stock (page 27) or clam juice
1/3 cup heavy cream or half-and-half
1 teaspoon dried dill
2 tablespoons chopped fresh basil or 1 tablespoon dried
Salt and pepper
1/4 cup dry white wine
1 tablespoon potato starch or cornstarch
About 1 tablespoon oil
1 1/4 pounds fresh or dried fettuccine

1. Preheat oven to 200°F. Rinse the fish, pat dry, and sprinkle lightly with salt. Heat a heavy cast-iron skillet until very hot, and rub lightly with oil. Add the fish and sear for about 2 minutes on each side. Transfer the skillet to the oven for 10 minutes, remove, let stand for 5 minutes, then cut fish into chunks or flake with 2 forks.

2. Meanwhile, heat the oil in a heavy 6-cup nonreactive saucepan, add the onion, cover, and cook for 3 minutes. Add the garlic, and red and yellow peppers, cover, and cook for 3 minutes. Meanwhile, slice and cut the mushrooms into strips, incorporate them into the vegetable sauce, and simmer 3 minutes, covered. Add the Fish Stock, cream, dill, and dried basil (reserve fresh basil). Cook for 5 minutes, uncovered, to reduce the liquid.

3. While the sauce is simmering, bring 6 quarts of water to a rolling boil, add a little salt and about 1 tablespoon of oil. Add a handful of fettuccine at a time. Once the water returns to a full boil, after about a minute, check a piece of the pasta for doneness. Do not overcook. (Dry fettuccine will require about 8 minutes.) Drain at once.
5. To finish the sauce, stir the wine into the potato starch to make a smooth paste; add to the sauce, remove the pan from the heat, and stir for about 1 minute to thicken slightly. Stir in the fish, taking care to break up the pieces as small as possible. Stir in the fresh basil.
6. Dish the fettuccine onto warm plates and spoon the sauce over the pasta. Serve at once.

Serves 6.

HINT   Potato starch produces a less starchy sauce than other thickeners, such as flour or cornstarch. Potato starch must be added at the right time in the cooking process, because it cannot be heated above 176°F. or it will lose its consistency and thin out. Look for potato starch in the Kosher section of your supermarket.

Penne with Smoked Fish Sauce

Penne is a short tubular-shaped pasta, always purchased dried. The word *penne* means pen in English, which makes sense because of its appearance. Sometimes it is marketed as *mostaccioli* (mustache), which does not make much sense. Nomenclature aside, this hearty pasta needs a vigorous, rich sauce to do it justice. If you can't find penne, other varieties of pasta, including dried ziti, paparadelle, or sea shells would all work well in this dish.

You can prepare the basic smoked fish sauce the day before; refrigerate as soon as it cools. The vegetables can be sautéed a few hours in advance and refrigerated. The sauce must be thickened at the last moment.

PREPARATION TIME   10 minutes
SMOKING   20 minutes
STANDING   3 hours
COOKING   15 minutes

Smoked fish

½ pound fish fillet with skin
   intact, such as bluefish, sea
   trout, salmon, or catfish

2 tablespoons black tea leaves
2 tablespoons brown sugar
1 crumbled bay leaf

1½ cup Fish Stock (page 27) or
   clam juice
½ cup dry white wine
3 tablespoons heavy cream
A pinch saffron thread
Freshly ground pepper to taste
2 tablespoons olive oil
¾ pound penne or other dried
   pasta
2 cloves garlic, peeled and minced
½ teaspoon dried oregano

½ red pepper, julienned (page 34)
   (about 1 cup)
2 medium zucchini, cut into
   match-sticks (page 34) (about 1
   cup)
¼ cup water
1 tablespoon potato starch or
   cornstarch
2 tablespoons chopped fresh
   parsley (optional)

1. Smoke the fish with its flavorings according to the directions for Quick-Smoked Trout Canapés (page 51). Cool, remove skin, flake, and reserve.

2. Pour the Fish Stock and white wine into a 6- to 8-cup nonreactive saucepot. Add 2 tablespoons of the cream, the saffron, and pepper to taste. Bring to a simmer and cook uncovered for 5 minutes. Add the smoked fish, simmer for another minute or so, then remove from the heat, cover, and set aside to stand for at least 3 hours. (This amount of standing time is necessary for the smoky flavor to penetrate the sauce.)

3. About 15 minutes before serving, boil water in a 3- or 4-quart pot. Add a large pinch of salt and a tablespoon of oil, if desired. Add the pasta slowly to maintain the water at the boiling point, and cook for 7 to 9 minutes. Test for doneness after 7 minutes. Drain at once and shake the colander sharply to eliminate any remaining water.

4. While the pasta is cooking, reheat the smoked fish sauce, adding the garlic and oregano; simmer slowly. Heat the remaining tablespoon of oil in a heavy 10-inch skillet. Sauté the red peppers and zucchini quickly over fairly high heat for about 2 or 3 minutes, until lightly browned but still slightly crisp. Remove with a skimmer and transfer to the simmering smoked fish sauce.

5. Mix the water with the potato starch to make a smooth paste and stir into the sauce. Remove sauce at once from the heat, add the remaining tablespoon of cream, and stir until the sauce has thickened a little.

6. Divide the pasta among 4 or 5 warm dishes and spoon the sauce over all. If you like, sprinkle with fresh parsley. Serve immediately.

Serves 4 or 5.

ON MAKING A RISOTTO

For many, making a successful risotto is a mysterious business. If you don't use the right rice, you'll end up with a gluey mess. If you don't stir constantly, the rice won't cook evenly. If the heat isn't precisely correct, the liquid will evaporate too fast or too slowly. And so on.

Relax. There *is* a bit of a ritual to making this Milanese specialty, but it is not the daunting chore that we often expect it to be. Some important points:

Rice

Italian *arborio* rice is preferred—no doubt about that. Its grains are short, round, and give up starch as they cook, thus creating a risotto with a creamy, delicate texture. Arborio can be purchased in specialty stores and in Italian markets. However, many Italian cooks living in the United States often use a commercially available converted long-grain rice instead of arborio, which is a more expensive rice and harder to get. Even though the long-grain rice does not expand quite as much as arborio does, it produces a very nice risotto.

Pot

Use a pot with a heavy bottom, so that it will retain the heat. You need a handle on the pot so that you can comfortably hold onto it as you stir.

Stirring

In most cookbooks, you are admonished *never* to stop stirring the risotto. Nonsense. You can stop, but not for long periods. The rice can bubble away for as much as 15 to 20 seconds unattended, while you, for instance, chop up parsley, cut up shrimp, or bring out the bowls.

Liquid

The precise quantity of liquid needed will vary, depending on the absorbing property of the rice. Stock must be added in small increments so that the rice is never swimming in liquid. It is also important to have about three-quarters of a cup of the stock reserved, which you stir into the rice *after* it is removed from the heat. This final addition of liquid helps to develop the extra creamy texture of the risotto.

Spoon

Use a wooden spoon. It's better at scraping up more of the rice on the bottom of the pot, and the wood is gentle on the rice grains.

One final word of encouragement: Although you are spending nearly 30 minutes hovering over the risotto, remember that you are preparing a *main* dish, which will feed some 4 to 6 people. A tasty, smooth risotto is well worth the time and effort.

Shrimp Risotto

Since most of the shrimp in this satisfying main course dish is cut up, you can buy the smaller variety and save money. Don't use olive oil instead of a vegetable oil in this dish; the heavier flavor of the olive oil masks the subtle taste of the risotto. Serve with a garden salad.

See page 167 for tips on making risotto.

PREPARATION TIME   40 minutes

COOKING   45 minutes

1¼ pounds small shrimp
2 quarts water
1 carrot, sliced
1 cup chopped onion
Salt and pepper
2 tablespoons butter or margarine
2 tablespoons vegetable oil
2 teaspoons chopped garlic (about 2 cloves)

2 tomatoes peeled, seeded, and chopped (page 34)
3 cups arborio or long-grain rice
½ cup dry white wine at room temperature
1 cup Chicken Stock (page 29) or canned broth
3 tablespoons chopped fresh parsley
6 parsley sprigs (optional)

1. Rinse the shrimp and peel. Reserve the shrimp and place the shells in a 3-quart pot. Add the water, carrot, ½ cup of the onion, and lightly season with salt and pepper. Bring to a boil, reduce heat, and simmer briskly for 20 to 30 minutes, uncovered. Strain the stock into a bowl and press the shells to extract all liquid. Discard shells. Rinse out the pot, return the stock to the pot, and place over low heat.
2. While the shrimp stock is cooking, prepare the shrimp. Reserve half the shrimp whole and cut the rest in half.
3. In a heavy pot, melt the butter with the oil, add the remaining ½ cup onion, and cook until almost translucent, 3 or 4 minutes. Add the garlic and tomatoes, and, while stirring, cook 30 seconds. Add the rice and cook for about 2 minutes, stirring constantly, until the grains turn opaque. Set the timer for 18 minutes.
4. Add the white wine to the pot and cook over high heat until the liquid has been absorbed, stirring almost constantly. Slowly add the

Chicken Stock, then the shrimp stock, ½ cup at a time. Stirring steadily, continue adding the liquids, waiting for the stock to be absorbed before adding the next half cup. Continue preparing the risotto in this manner until a good part of the stock has been absorbed.

5. When the timer rings, stop adding the shrimp stock and put aside the remaining ½ to ¾ cup. Add the halved shrimp to the rice and season with salt and pepper. Taste for an al dente (slightly firm) texture. Keep on a low heat.

6. Wipe a small skillet with an oiled paper towel, heat thoroughly, and sauté the reserved 6 whole shrimp until they are dark pink and lightly browned on both sides; about 30 seconds.

7. Remove the cooked risotto from the heat, add the chopped parsley, and most or all of the reserved shrimp stock. Add and stir until the rice grains are moist and creamy.

8. Spoon the risotto into 6 heated bowls. Garnish each with a shrimp and a sprig of parsley, if desired. Serve at once.

Serves 6.

Scallop and Spinach Risotto

This is a delicate and subtle risotto. The velvety texture of the tiny white scallops is a nice contrast to the rice.

See page 167 for tips on making risotto.

PREPARATION TIME   19 minutes
COOKING   20 minutes

3 tablespoons butter or margarine
1 tablespoon vegetable oil
4 scallions, chopped
1 celery rib, chopped
3 cups rice, preferably arborio
3 cups Chicken Stock (page 29) or canned broth
4½ cups Fish Stock (page 27) or clam juice

1 cup dry white wine at room temperature
½ pound whole leaf spinach, washed, stemmed, and shredded
½ cup half-and-half
¾ pound bay scallops
Salt and pepper

1. Melt 2 tablespoons of the butter or margarine with the oil in a heavy 3-quart casserole. Add the scallions and celery, cover, and cook for 5 minutes. Add the rice and cook for about 2 minutes, constantly stirring, until the grains turn opaque and are coated with the butter and oil. Meanwhile, in another 3-quart saucepot, heat the Fish Stock and Chicken Stock together to the boiling point.
2. Set the timer for 18 minutes. Add the white wine to the rice mixture and cook over medium heat until all the liquid has been absorbed. Stir often. Ladle in a cupful of the combined stocks and stir often until absorbed. Continue adding more hot stock in the same manner.
3. Stir the rice intermittently while preparing the spinach and scallop sauce. Melt the remaining tablespoon of butter or margarine in a deep skillet or pot, add the spinach with water clinging to it, cover, and steam for about 1 minute, or until the leaves are almost completely collapsed but still a vivid green. Add the cream and cook briefly, stirring. Remove pot from the heat, add the scallops, season with salt and pepper, and mix together. Cover and put aside.

4. When the timer rings, begin tasting the rice for an al dente (slightly firm) texture and season with salt and pepper. When rice is done, stop adding the stocks, reserving about ¾ cup. Spoon about three-fourths of the scallop-spinach sauce into the rice, mix, and taste again for seasonings. Correct, if necessary. Remove from heat and stir in the reserved stock until rice is moist and creamy.
5. Spoon the risotto into 6 heated bowls and garnish each with a spoonful of the reserved spinach-scallop sauce. Serve at once.

Serves 6.

Monkfish Risotto in Red Wine Sauce

This is an unusual risotto, flavored by herbs, lemon, and a touch of wine. If you need more liquid before the rice is cooked, add a little water or wine instead of the fish stock. Use the fish stock for the final addition of liquid when the rice is removed from the heat.

See page 167 for tips on cooking risotto.

PREPARATION TIME   20 minutes
COOKING   25 minutes

2 tablespoons oil
¼ cup chopped onion
1 clove garlic, peeled and minced
1½ cups arborio or long-grain rice
3 cups Fish Stock (page 27) or 2 cups clam broth and 1 cup water
1 cup peeled, seeded, and chopped tomato (page 34)

1 cup light red wine
¼ teaspoon fresh or dried rosemary
Salt and pepper
½ to ¾ pound monkfish, cut into ½-inch pieces
2 tablespoons chopped fresh parsley, preferably Italian parsley
1 teaspoon grated lemon peel
4 parsley sprigs and 1 lemon slice, cut into quarters, for garnish

1. In a heavy 4- or 5-quart pot, heat the oil and add the onion. Cover and cook for 3 minutes, or until soft and translucent. Add the garlic and cook for 30 seconds, stirring. Add the rice and cook for 2 minutes, stirring constantly until the grains turn opaque. Set the timer for 18 minutes. Reserve ¾ cup Fish Stock.
2. Add ½ cup of the Fish Stock and cook over medium heat until it has been absorbed, stirring almost constantly. Stir in the chopped tomato and the juices and cook until the liquid has been almost completely absorbed.
3. Stir in half the red wine, the rosemary, and salt and pepper, and cook until the wine has been absorbed. Slowly add the remaining wine and Fish Stock, stirring steadily and waiting for the stock to be absorbed before adding the next half cup. Continue cooking the risotto in this manner until almost all the Fish Stock has been absorbed.

4. When the timer rings, add the monkfish pieces and begin tasting soon for an al dente (slightly firm) texture. When the rice is done, stop adding the liquid.
5. Remove the cooked risotto from the heat, add the chopped parsley, grated lemon peel, and reserved fish stock, and stir until the rice grains are moist and creamy.
6. Spoon the risotto into 6 heated bowls and garnish each with a parsley sprig and lemon wedge.

Serves 4.

HINT   Grate lemon or orange peel, using a small grater, onto a dish or a piece of wax paper. Use a stiff vegetable brush to retrieve the rind caught in the teeth of the grater.

Pizzas and Pies

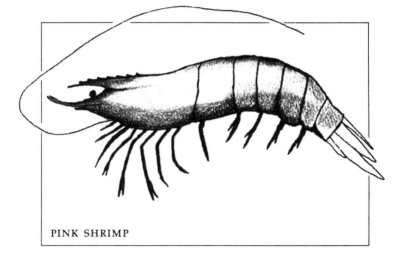

PINK SHRIMP

Pastry is the unifying theme in this chapter. There are several varieties, besides the traditional flour-based type. For example, a cornmeal crust lies under the Shrimp Pie, while mashed potatoes cover a hearty seafood dish. Simple pita bread envelops a hearty fish filling, and *kulebyaka*, the famous Russian salmon loaf, is all wrapped up in a rich, extravagantly decorated pastry.

With pizzas, of course, the process is reversed. It's the dough that gets covered up with many different kinds of fish. Who says pizza only has to have sausage and pepperoni?

Pizza Dough

Several recipes in this section require the making of dough for pizza, hence its inclusion here. This particular recipe calls for the use of a food processor, although you can prepare the dough by hand. For super-fast dough, buy frozen bread dough and keep it in the freezer. The usual package contains two 1-pound loaves, and each is enough for a 14-inch pizza. The bread is not as tasty as freshly made dough; you sacrifice some flavor and texture for convenience.

PREPARATION TIME   5 minutes

RISING   about 1 hour

2 cups all-purpose flour
1 package (1 tablespoon) dry yeast*
¼ teaspoon salt

¾ cup water
1 tablespoon olive oil

1. Put the flour, yeast, and salt in a food processor and pulse a few times to aerate the flour. Meanwhile, heat the water to 120°F. (or use very hot tap water), add the olive oil, and pour into the processor with the motor running. Stop the motor when the dough forms a ball. Oil a mixing bowl, drop the dough into it, cover, and place in a warm spot to rise for about 1 hour, or until doubled in bulk.
2. Preheat oven to 425°F. Put the dough on a floured board, knead for 1 minute, and shape into a ball.
3. Oil a pizza pan, place the dough on it, and, with oiled hands, spread the dough to cover the surface of the pan, making a thicker crust around the edge. A 12-inch pan will have a baked crust of almost ½-inch thick; a 14-inch pan will have a thin crust. Top with garnishes and bake for 10 to 15 minutes, or until the crust is crisp and the topping is piping hot.

Makes one 12- to 14-inch pizza.

HINT   An extra crunch can be added to pizza dough by adding 1 tablespoon cornmeal to the dough before the final kneading (Step 2). After greasing the pizza pan, sprinkle with a little cornmeal, then proceed with stretching the dough.

*Fast-rising yeasts may also be used. The rising time would be cut in half, to about 30 minutes.

Shrimp and Spinach Pizza

This is a colorful, tasty pizza that can double as a main dish entrée or, sliced, as an appetizer. Frozen spinach, which only needs to be thawed and squeezed, is preferred over fresh in this recipe, and, since most of the shrimp is cut up, buy the less expensive smaller variety.

PREPARATION TIME   20 minutes, plus dough
BAKING   about 15 minutes

1 recipe Pizza Dough (page 176),
  or 1 pound frozen bread dough,
  defrosted
1 cup low-fat ricotta*
½ pound small shrimp, peeled
Salt and pepper
About 2 tablespoons olive oil
¼ pound mushrooms, sliced

One 10-ounce package frozen
  whole-leaf spinach, thawed
4 scallions, each cut into 3 or 4
  pieces
½ tablespoon Pesto (page 32)
6 ounces low-fat mozzarella
  cheese, shredded

1. Reserve 4 of the most attractive shrimp and cut the rest into ¼-inch pieces. Put the cut-up shrimp in a small bowl, and season with a little salt and pepper and ½ tablespoon olive oil. Mix to coat all the pieces and put aside.
2. Meanwhile, heat a skillet, add 1 teaspoon of the olive oil and the mushrooms. Cook over high heat to brown a little and eliminate any moisture; cook, covered, for about 30 seconds. Uncover and season with salt and pepper. Remove the mushrooms with a skimmer and reserve.
3. Thoroughly squeeze out the water from the spinach, pull apart, and put in a food processor. Add the scallions and pulse a few times to coarsely chop the vegetables. Add the ricotta, Pesto, and freshly ground pepper and process for a few seconds. Do not purée the mixture; there should be a chunky texture to this pizza topping. (The vegetables may be chopped by hand.)
4. Preheat oven to 450°F. Oil a 14-inch pizza pan, place the dough on it, and, with oiled hands, spread the dough to cover the surface of the pan, making a thicker crust around the edge. Spread the spinach

mixture over the dough. (A wet rubber spatula works well.) Scatter the sautéed mushrooms over the spinach bed, then the shrimp pieces. Sprinkle the mozzarella over the top, making certain to cover all the shrimp. Reserve a pinch of the cheese. Bake for 12 minutes.

5. Meanwhile, put the 4 reserved whole shrimp in the bowl used for the shrimp pieces. Turn them over to coat with the residual oil in the dish. Remove pizza from oven, place the 4 shrimp in the center in a spiral pattern, and drop the pinch of reserved cheese in the center. Return the pizza to the oven for another 3 or 4 minutes, or until the shrimp are cooked and the crust is nicely brown.

6. Let the pizza rest for 2 or 3 minutes before cutting it into wedges. Makes one 14-inch pizza.

Serves 4 to 6.

*Different brands of ricotta contain varying amounts of water. If the ricotta you are using seems to contain a lot of liquid, scrape the cheese into a strainer suspended over a bowl. Let the ricotta drain while you continue the recipe.

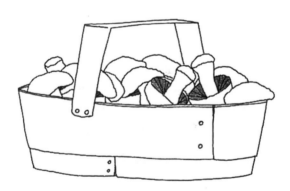

Mussel Pizza

You can substitute fresh soft-shell clams in this recipe, if you prefer. Either mollusk brings a mild briny taste to this savory pizza.

PREPARATION TIME   40 minutes, plus dough
BAKING   15 minutes

1 recipe Pizza Dough (page 176), or 1 pound frozen bread dough, defrosted
2 pounds mussels, scrubbed and cleaned
1 tablespoon olive oil
1 medium onion, sliced
¼ pound mushrooms, sliced

2 cups peeled, seeded, and chopped tomatoes (page 34), or one 1-pound can whole tomatoes
¼ teaspoon dried oregano
Freshly ground pepper to taste
8 ounces part skim milk mozzarella, shredded

1. While the dough is rising, steam the mussels (page 17). Strain and reserve the cooking broth. Heat the oil in a heavy 6-cup nonreactive saucepot. Add the onion, cover, and cook for 5 minutes. Add the mushrooms, cover, and cook for another 5 minutes. Transfer the cooked vegetables to a bowl.
2. Use the same pot for cooking the sauce. Add the tomatoes, 1 cup of the mussel broth, oregano, and a generous grinding of pepper. Bring to a boil and, stirring occasionally, simmer for about 15 or 20 minutes, until the liquid is reduced and the sauce is quite thick. (If using canned tomatoes, crush them against the sides of the pot when stirring.) The sauce should be reduced to about 1½ cups.
3. Preheat oven to 450°F. Oil a 14-inch pizza pan, place the dough on it, and, with oiled hands, spread the dough to cover the surface of the pan, making a thicker crust around the edge. Spread the tomato sauce on the pizza dough, then scatter the onion-mushroom mixture over it. Scatter the mussels over the top and sprinkle the mozzarella over all. Take care that all the mussels are covered with the cheese to protect them from the high oven heat, which might toughen them.
4. Bake the pizza for about 15 minutes, or until the cheese is lightly browned and bubbly.

5. Let the pizza rest for 5 minutes before cutting it into wedges. Makes one 14-inch pizza.

Serves 4 to 6.

Tuna and Vegetable Pizza

Now that fresh tuna is available almost the year round, we can use it in a variety of ways, even as a topping for pizza. This is a rich, tasty main dish entrée or appetizer.

The vegetable sauce can be prepared in advance, even the day before, and be refrigerated until needed.

PREPARATION TIME   20 minutes, plus dough
CHILLING   30 minutes
BAKING   15 minutes

1 recipe Pizza Dough (page 176),
    or 1 pound frozen bread dough,
    defrosted
½ pound tuna steak or swordfish
2 tablespoons olive oil
3 scallions, sliced
1 cup canned plum tomatoes (6 or
    7), drained and chopped
¼ pound mushrooms, sliced

¼ pound zucchini, shredded
3 anchovy fillets*
¼ cup sun-dried tomatoes,
    chopped
¼ cup dry white wine
Freshly ground pepper to taste
1 tablespoon cornmeal
6 ounces part skim milk
    mozzarella, shredded

1. To firm the tuna for slicing, tightly cover it with plastic wrap and put in the freezer for about 30 minutes. Remove and cut into thin slices.
2. Heat the oil in a skillet and add the scallions, tomatoes, mushrooms, zucchini, anchovies, dried tomatoes, and white wine. Cover and cook over medium heat for 5 minutes. Uncover and cook over high heat for 10 minutes, or until most of the juices have evaporated.
3. Preheat oven to 450°F. Oil a 14-inch pizza pan, place the dough on it, and, with oiled fingers, spread the dough to cover the surface of the pan, making a thicker crust around the edge. Brush the remaining tablespoon olive oil over the dough, then sprinkle with the cornmeal. Spread the vegetable mixture evenly over the dough, then top with a layer of the tuna slices. Sprinkle the mozzarella over the fish, making certain to cover all of the fish. Bake for 15 minutes.
4. Let the pizza rest for 5 to 10 minutes before cutting it into wedges. Makes one 14-inch pizza.

Serves 4 to 6.

*Anchovies dissolve easily in hot liquid and intensify the fish flavor in stews and sauces. Rinse them first to eliminate as much oil and salt as possible.

Shrimp Pie in a Cornmeal Crust

Although a regular pastry crust can be used for this delicately flavored pie, I find that the combination of cornmeal and ricotta works especially well with the shrimp. Since most of the shrimp will be cut up, buy the most economical size (usually the smallest) at the market. A 15-ounce container of ricotta, instead of the full 16-ounce measure, will also work in this recipe.

The cornmeal crust can be prepared in advance, but it must be spread into the greased pie dish while it is hot. Brush the crust with oil to keep it from drying out. You can also make the filling a day before, cover closely, and refrigerate until ready to bake.

PREPARATION TIME   25 minutes

CHILLING   40 minutes

COOKING   about 40 minutes

2 cups ricotta, preferably low-fat
1 cup yellow cornmeal
2 cups cold water
1 teaspoon ground coriander
½ teaspoon sugar
¼ teaspoon salt
2 teaspoons butter or margarine,
    softened
1 tablespoon dry white wine
1 teaspoon anchovy paste
½ pound small shrimp, peeled

1 tomato, peeled, seeded, and
    chopped (page 34)
2 scallions, chopped
2 to 3 teaspoons Pesto (page 32)
Pepper
2 egg whites
1 tablespoon cornstarch
2 tablespoons grated fresh
    Parmesan cheese
2 parsley sprigs

1. If the ricotta seems watery, put it in a strainer and suspend over a bowl to drain off excess liquid. Put the cornmeal in a small mixing bowl and add 1 cup of the cold water. Stir with a whisk into a smooth paste. Pour the remaining cup water in a 2- to 2½-quart pot and add the coriander, sugar, and salt. Bring to a boil, and, while whisking, pour in the cornmeal mixture.* Reduce the heat to medium and cook about 3 to 4 minutes, whisking often, until the cornmeal mush is very thick. Meanwhile, use the butter or margarine to liberally grease a 6-cup deep pie dish. Scoop the cornmeal mush into the dish, allow to cool for

a minute or two, then use a rubber spatula to push the hot mush into a thick shell against the sides of the dish. Do not extend the mush into a decorative rim above the sides. If the spatula sticks, wipe it with oil. Cool the shell for 10 minutes, then brush with oil. Refrigerate for at least 30 minutes.

2. Meanwhile, in a small 1- or 2-cup pot, boil the white wine and anchovy paste. Scrape into a small cup and set aside to cool. Reserve 3 of the shrimp and cut the rest into ¼-inch pieces; do not chop. Rub the reserved whole shrimp with oil and tightly wrap in aluminum foil; reserve.

3. Preheat oven to 375°F. In a bowl, mix the drained ricotta, tomato, scallions, 2 teaspoons of the Pesto, the pepper, and the anchovy paste mixture. If desired, add the additional teaspoon Pesto. Stir in the egg whites and cornstarch, then finally the shrimp pieces. Spoon the filling into the cornmeal shell, smooth the top with a spatula, and sprinkle with the grated cheese. Bake for 35 to 40 minutes, or until a small sharp knife inserted into the center comes out almost dry. Remove the pie from the oven and let stand for 10 minutes.

4. During the last 5 minutes of baking time, put the foil package of shrimp in the oven. Remove with the pie. If the shrimp seem slightly underdone, rewrap and return to the hot oven for a few minutes more.

5. Let the pie rest for 5 minutes before cutting. Place the 3 whole shrimp upright in the center and tuck the parsley sprigs in the middle. Cut the pie into wedges and lift out with a spatula, reaching well under the cornmeal crust to detach.

Serves 6.

*When making cornmeal mush, always mix the cornmeal with water to form a thin paste *before* adding it to boiling water. This precaution reduces the chance of lumps forming in the cornmeal.

Bluefish Pie

Because of the hearty taste and texture of bluefish, a mere half pound will amply serve five or six when it is baked in a pie. The pastry used here is less rich and caloric than most, and, since almost no water is used, the crust is exceptionally tender.

PREPARATION TIME   25 minutes
COOKING   45 minutes

Pastry for one 9-inch top crust

1¼ cups sifted flour
¼ teaspoon salt
½ teaspoon dry mustard

1 large egg at room temperature
3 tablespoons butter, melted and
  cooled

½ pound bluefish
2 medium turnips, peeled (about
  ¼ pound)
3 carrots, peeled and sliced
2 tablespoons oil
1 medium onion, sliced in half
  vertically, then sliced crosswise
1 celery rib, sliced

2 tablespoons flour
2 tablespoons ketchup
1 cup Beef Stock (pages 29–30) or
  canned beef broth
1 bay leaf
Pepper
1 tablespoon chopped pimiento

1. To make pastry, place the sifted flour in a mixing bowl and stir in the salt and dry mustard. Beat the egg in a small bowl or cup, add the melted butter, and beat again. Stir egg-and-butter mixture into the flour, mixing with a fork until the flour is absorbed by the liquid. Moisten your fingers by scraping them around the inside of the bowl used for the egg and butter. Work the dough lightly with your moistened fingers until it forms a ball. No water should be necessary, but if you find the dough too dry, add only the amount of water absolutely necessary to make the pastry hold together.
2. Lightly flour a work surface and, with the heel of your hand, push small pieces of the dough away from you, pushing them to about 6 inches in length. Re-form the dough and repeat. This thoroughly blends the fat and flour together. Re-form the dough into a smooth

ball, cover with wax paper, and let the dough rest for 15 minutes. Do not refrigerate.

3. Meanwhile, steam the bluefish (page 24). Once cooked and cool, remove all bones and flake the fish into 1-inch chunks.

4. While the fish is steaming, cut the turnips into quarters and cook until tender. Using the same pot, cook the carrots, but do not cook the 2 vegetables together.

5. Preheat oven to 400°F. Heat the oil in a 6-cup saucepot, add the onion and celery, cover, and cook for 10 minutes. Stir in the flour and ketchup and cook for about 1 minute. Add the Beef Stock, bay leaf, and pepper, cover, and simmer for 5 minutes. Add the turnips and carrots and mix well. Gently stir in the bluefish and pimiento. Remove the bay leaf and spoon the filling into a deep 9-inch pie dish that can hold 4 cups.

6. Roll out the pastry on a floured surface, fold in half, and make 3 slashes in the center of the fold. Transfer the pastry to the pie dish, place it over filling, and press onto the edges of the dish. Wet the perimeter of the dough, fold the dough over to make an edge, and crimp in a fluted pattern.

7. Place the pie on a baking sheet and bake for 15 minutes. Reduce the heat to 350°F., and bake 15 minutes more. Remove from the oven and let rest for 10 minutes.

8. Cut the pie into V-shaped portions with large serving spoons.

Serves 5 or 6.

Monkfish and Sprouts in Pita

Technically, this is a sandwich. But since the spicy filling is enveloped with bread, it seems to belong here. Whatever the category, it's a treat, whether for a casual dinner or as a luncheon surprise.

PREPARATION TIME 15 minutes

MARINATING 15 minutes

COOKING 3 minutes

½ pound monkfish, cut into strips, ¼- to ½-inch wide

½ cup dry red wine

1 teaspoon ground cumin*

Salt and pepper

2 jalapeño peppers

½ pound bean sprouts, rinsed and shaken dry

2 garlic cloves, peeled and minced

¼ cup red wine vinegar

6 mini-size (4-inch) whole wheat pita breads

1. Stir the red wine, cumin, and salt and pepper into a bowl. Add the monkfish strips and stir gently to moisten all surfaces of the fish. Put aside to marinate for 15 minutes.
2. Meanwhile, prepare the jalapeños according to the directions on page 35. Cut into long slivers.
3. Lift the monkfish out of the marinade, reserving it, and dry the fish on paper towels. Heat the oil in a 9- or 10-inch nonreactive skillet. When the oil is quite hot, add the fish slices. Sauté for about a minute while turning them over a few times with a spatula. Lift the fish strips out of the skillet and reserve in a bowl.
4. Put the sprouts, garlic, and jalapeño strips into the same skillet and season with salt and pepper. Cover and cook for 30 seconds. Add the marinade, cover, and cook 30 seconds. Return the monkfish to the skillet to heat. Sprinkle on the vinegar, simmer all for a few seconds, cover, and turn off the heat.
5. Toast the pita breads and make a wide slit in each. Spoon the filling into the breads and serve at once.

Serves 6.

*For a richer cumin flavor, buy whole cumin seeds and toast them in a small cast-iron skillet over low heat for about 10 minutes, until the seeds turn a dark cocoa color. Remove from skillet, cool, then store in a tightly sealed jar. Whenever a recipe calls for ground cumin, grind as much as you need in an electric mini-grinder.

Kulebyaka

(RUSSIAN SALMON LOAF IN PASTRY)

This classic dish takes some time to make, but it is not difficult to put together. Its appearance and rich flavor make this decorative loaf a special treat. This is party fare, and it will be long remembered by family and guests.

PREPARATION TIME   about 1 hour

CHILLING   1 hour

BAKING   about 1 hour

Pastry

4 cups flour, plus flour for pastry board

10 tablespoons diced and chilled, or solid vegetable shortening

1 teaspoon salt

2 eggs, chilled

6 to 8 tablespoons cold water

2 tablespoons butter or margarine

1 onion, chopped (about 1 cup)

½ cup kasha (toasted buckwheat kernels)

½ cup uncooked rice

2 cups Chicken Stock (page 29) or canned chicken broth

Salt and pepper

½ pound mushrooms, chopped

¼ cup dry vermouth

4 teaspoons chopped fresh dill or 3 teaspoons dried

1 pound salmon

2 to 3 cups Fish Stock (page 27)

2 eggs

½ cup sour cream

2 tablespoons melted butter or margarine

4 tablespoons melted butter or margarine, with 1 teaspoon dill (optional)

1. To make pastry,* put the flour, lard or shortening, and salt in the food processor. Use the on/off switch to cut the lard into pieces. If necessary, let the motor run a few seconds to produce a mealy texture. Beat the eggs with 2 tablespoons of water, and, with the motor running, pour into the bowl. Add water, a tablespoon at a time, until the dough begins to cohere. Stop the machine after each water addition, gather a little of the dough with your fingertips, and press it gently; if it stays together, it is ready. Do not let the machine

pull the dough into a ball; it will overdevelop the gluten in the flour and toughen the pastry.

2. By hand, gather the dough into a loose ball, and transfer it to a lightly floured pastry board. With the heel of your hand, push small pieces of it away from you, pushing about 6 inches. Re-form the dough and repeat. Gather the dough into a ball, cover closely with plastic wrap, and chill for at least 1 hour. The pastry will keep in the refrigerator for several days.

3. Melt the butter or margarine in a large skillet, add the onion, cover, and cook over low heat for 5 minutes. Add the kasha and rice, increase heat to medium, and stir. Cook for 2 or 3 minutes, or until the rice turns opaque. Add the Chicken Stock and a little salt and pepper, cover, lower the heat, and simmer for 5 minutes. Stir the chopped mushrooms into the rice mixture with the vermouth. Add 2 teaspoons of the dill. Cover and cook for 5 minutes. Remove cover, fluff the grains with a fork, and transfer to a mixing bowl. Cool and refrigerate.

4. Poach the salmon according to the directions for Cold Salmon Soup (page 89), using 2 to 3 cups Fish Stock. Let cool and remove all skin and bones from the salmon. Break into chunks.

5. Preheat oven to 450°F. Beat 1 of the eggs with the sour cream, season lightly with salt and pepper, and add to the grain and mushroom mixture. Stir well to incorporate the cream completely into the filling. Stir the remaining 2 teaspoons dill into the melted butter.

6. Roll out the pastry on a well-floured board into a rectangle, approximately 18 × 12 inches. (It should be twice as thick as for a tart.) Trim the edges of the dough to make the rectangle even; reserve the scraps. Transfer the dough to a heavily greased baking sheet.

7. Use about one-third of the grain-mushroom filling to make a rectangle about 8 × 4 inches in the center of the dough. Scatter half the salmon chunks over the filling, then dribble half the dill butter over the salmon. Make another layer of filling, salmon, and dill butter, finishing the loaf with the remaining grain-mushroom filling. Keep patting the fish loaf at the sides to keep them firm and straight.

8. Cut out a small rectangle of dough (about 4 × 3 inches) from each of the 4 corners, taking care not to reach all the way to the filling. (Add the cut-outs to leftover dough.) Brush well-beaten egg all over the dough, and bring 1 long side up over the filling; brush with egg.

Bring the other long side up and finally the 2 shorter ends to completely enclose the filling. Brush with egg at each step.

9. Using some of the leftover dough, take pieces of it and rub them between your floured hands to form a rope; tuck this rope close in at the base of the loaf, all around, thus providing a support for the heavy filling. Brush this foundation with egg. Decorate the loaf with remaining leftover dough, cut into scalloped circles, or simply score lightly with the tip of a sharp knife. Brush entire surface with egg and cut out 2 holes about 3 inches from each end. Make 2 chimneys from parchment paper or aluminum foil and put into the holes.

10. Place in oven. When the dough begins to appear to firm up and change color a little (about 10 to 15 minutes), reduce heat to 375°F. and bake for about 45 minutes, or until the crust is nicely browned. Test internal heat with a thermometer; it should read 140°F. Remove from oven, remove parchment paper or foil, and allow to rest for 30 minutes before slicing. Pass melted butter with dill as a sauce, if desired.

Serves 10 to 12 as main course.

---

*Alternative method for preparing pastry by hand: Put the flour on a pastry board. Make a well in the center and in it put the salt, lard or shortening, egg, and 2 tablespoons of water. Mix these ingredients well with your fingertips, gradually incorporating the flour until the mixture becomes mealy. Add water, a little at a time, until the pastry holds together. Continue with Step 2.

Seafood Pie with a Potato Crust

This hearty dish is a cousin of shepherd's pie, that tasty disguise for leftover meats. And, indeed, leftover fish can be used for this deep-dish pie, but it is good enough to merit your steaming a piece of fish specially for it. Don't feel bound to use just one kind of fish, however. Toss in a few shrimp, scallops, or mussels, and create an even more interesting combination.

The fish can be cooked the day before, as can the sauce and the mashed potatoes. Refrigerate the three items separately, then combine and reheat the sauce with the fish. If the potatoes are cold, flatten them a little before placing on top of the filling.

PREPARATION TIME   25 minutes
COOKING   10 minutes
BAKING   about 35 minutes

1 pound potatoes
3 tablespoons butter or margarine
3 cloves garlic, peeled and
   chopped
4 scallions, chopped
About ¼ cup milk
Salt and pepper
1½ pounds halibut, cod, pollock,
   or flounder
2 tablespoons oil
1 celery rib, chopped
1 medium onion, chopped

¼ pound mushrooms, sliced
¼ cup flour
1 tablespoon prepared mustard
1½ cups Fish Stock (page 27) or
   clam juice
¼ cup heavy cream or half-and-
   half
⅛ teaspoon cayenne
1 bay leaf
½ cup cooked peas, fresh or
   frozen
Paprika for sprinkling

1. Peel and slice the potatoes and in a saucepan of boiling water to cover boil for about 10 minutes, or until very soft. Drain, put in a bowl, and add 1 tablespoon of the butter or margarine, one-third of the garlic, and half the scallions. Mash thoroughly but do not over-purée, since there should be some texture to the potatoes. Stir in ¼ cup milk. (If the potatoes seem a bit dry, add another tablespoon or so of milk but do not make too soft.) Season with salt and pepper and reserve.
2. Meanwhile, either poach the fish (page 24) or steam it according to the

directions on page 24. If you poach the fish in milk, reserve the poaching liquid for the sauce. Flake the fish.

3. Preheat oven to 350°F. Melt the remaining 2 tablespoons of butter or margarine and the oil in an 8-cup saucepot. Add the celery and onion, stir, cover, and cook for 3 minutes. Add the remaining garlic, scallions, and mushrooms, cover, and simmer 2 minutes. Stir in the flour and mustard and stir until thick and smooth. Pour in about ½ cup Fish Stock and whisk until thick and smooth. Slowly pour in the remaining stock. (If milk was reserved from poaching the fish, substitute it for some of the Fish Stock.) Stir in the cream and season with the cayenne, salt and pepper, and bay leaf. Cover and simmer for 5 minutes. Remove the bay leaf and add the peas. Gently stir in the fish — try not to break it into small pieces.

5. Have ready an 8- to 10-cup soufflé dish or a similar deep dish. (A smaller dish is likely to bubble over a little in the oven, but a piece of aluminum foil placed under the dish would prevent any mess. A larger dish would not be filled to the top, and there would be no risk of bubbling over.) Pour in the filling and cover with the reserved mashed potatoes. Use a fork to spread the potatoes and to give an uneven crust. Sprinkle with paprika and bake for 25 to 30 minutes, or until the top is lightly browned. For deeper color, you may want to slip the pie under the broiler for a few seconds.

6. Let the pie rest for 5 minutes before serving, then serve directly from the dish with spoons. Put the potato crust on one side of the plate and the filling beside it.

Serves 6 to 8.

CHAPTER SEVEN

Salads

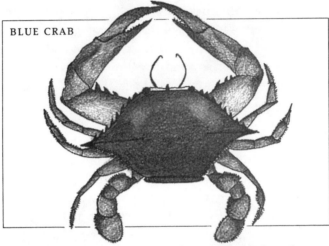

BLUE CRAB

Salads were once eaten primarily for health benefits or as a means of weight control. No more. Salads are now enjoyed for themselves and for their artful blend of fresh meat, fish, vegetable, and fruit products. Today a main dish salad is not a matter of virtue but a taste adventure.

Chefs have especially seized upon fresh fish to create salads of exceptional appeal. Cooks at home can also create interesting salads using many types of fish—from old favorites, such as shrimp and crabmeat salads, to intriguing combinations of fish and fruit, or fish and vegetable preparations. Wonderful in summer, these salads can also make a colorful, appetizing meal in the cooler months, augmented by a bowl of steaming homemade soup and a loaf of crusty bread.

Super Shrimp Salad

America has long had a love affair with shrimp salad. It is a summertime staple across the land and can be enjoyed in other seasons, too. This classic version is impressive enough for a light summer dinner or a special lunch.

PREPARATION TIME 20 minutes
COOKING 20 minutes
CHILLING 1 hour

1 medium to large potato

Court bouillon

6 cups water
1 cup dry white wine
1 onion, sliced
1 carrot, sliced
1 celery rib, sliced

1 bay leaf, broken in half
2 cloves garlic, peeled and
*   smashed (page 36)*
1 lemon, halved

1 pound shrimp in the shells
½ cup diced celery

½ cup diced seedless cucumber
*   with skin, or regular cucumber,*
*   peeled, seeded, and diced*

Dressing

1 cup mayonnaise
1½ tablespoons ketchup
2 teaspoons brandy

2 teaspoons lemon juice
A few drops hot red pepper sauce
Salt and pepper to taste

6 or 7 large lettuce leaves
1 tomato

8 black olives, Niçoise or
*   Kalamata*

1. Scrub the potato and boil in a pan of water to cover until tender, about 15 minutes. Drain at once, cool, and refrigerate. Meanwhile, put all court bouillon ingredients in a 2½- to 3-quart nonreactive pot, squeezing the juice from the lemon and tossing the lemon shell in as well. Bring to a boil, cover the pot, and simmer the liquid for 15 minutes.

2. Add the shrimp to the court bouillon, stir briefly, cover, and remove from the heat. Check after about 45 seconds — small shrimp should be just cooked through. Larger shrimp may need another 30 seconds. Drain at once and cool under cold running water. Peel the shrimp, reserve 2 whole (preferably with tails intact), and cut the rest into ½-inch pieces. Put the shrimp in a large mixing bowl.

3. Add the celery and cucumber to the shrimp. Peel and dice the potato and add it to the salad. Toss gently and chill the salad for at least 45 minutes.

4. Meanwhile, whisk together all the dressing ingredients. Cut the lettuce into chiffonade (page 34).

5. Pour the dressing over the salad and toss gently. Make a bed of about 1 cup chiffonade on each of 4 plates. Mound shrimp salad in the center. Cut the tomato into 8 wedges and place 2 of them at the top of each plate with 2 black olives between them. Slice the reserved shrimp in half and place in the center of each salad.

Serves 4.

Summer Fish Salad

A good fish salad is a welcome addition to summertime menus. However, it shouldn't be a bland or timid affair if you want to awaken flagging appetites. Here is an easy fish salad to prepare on a hot day. Fresh Vegetable Salsa (page 112) makes a colorful and piquant garnish for this dish.

PREPARATION TIME   15 minutes

COOKING   about 6 minutes, plus rice

CHILLING   at least 2 hours

1 pound fish fillets, such as
  flounder, turbot, cod, or halibut
2 cups low-fat milk
½ small onion, sliced
1 small bay leaf

Salt and pepper
2 cups cooked rice, chilled
⅓ cup chopped fresh parsley
Lettuce leaves

Sauce

1 cup mayonnaise
3 tablespoons lemon juice
1 clove garlic, peeled and chopped
2 anchovy fillets, plus 2 teaspoons
  anchovy oil
½ tablespoon capers

1 tablespoon chopped basil,
  preferably fresh
½ teaspoon whiskey
1 teaspoon light soy sauce
Salt and pepper

Black olives, cherry tomatoes,
  and 2 anchovy fillets
  for garnish (optional)

1. Lay the fish fillets in a nonreactive pan and pour in enough milk to just cover. Separate the onion slices into rings and scatter them over the fish. Break the bay leaf in half and add to the milk, then sprinkle with salt and pepper.
2. Cover the pan and put over medium heat. Slowly bring the milk to a simmer, reduce the heat, and cook very slowly for about 6 minutes, or until the fish is quite firm but not cooked through; it will continue to

cook as it cools in the milk. When completely cooled, lift the fish out
of the milk and flake into a bowl. Chill.

3. Put all the sauce ingredients in a blender or food processor and purée.
4. Once the fish is chilled, add to the rice and toss gently. Pour on the
   sauce, add the parsley, and mix thoroughly, but gently.
5. On a platter, arrange the fish salad in a mound on the lettuce leaves
   and decorate with the garnishes, if using, crisscrossing the anchovy
   fillets on top.

Serves 4.

HINT   Capers, the pickled unopened buds of a trailing shrub, add a spark
of flavor and piquancy to many dishes. The best capers are gathered
before they have fully developed, hence are quite small in size. Avoid
buying capers that are too green or too large (they should be smaller than
watermelon seeds), because they are of inferior quality and often are not
from a true caper shrub.

It is advisable to rinse the brine and vinegar from the capers before
using, thus freshening their flavor and reducing the sodium content.

Crabmeat Maison

The star of this salad is succulent crabmeat, with just enough additional flavorings to accent its sweetness. Enjoy this classic dish as a main course in the summer or as an impressive first course.

PREPARATION TIME   8 minutes
STANDING   15 to 30 minutes

Sauce

¼ cup mayonnaise
2 tablespoons fresh lemon juice
2 tablespoons capers, including
 brine

1 scallion, very thinly sliced
1 tablespoon chopped fresh parsley
Freshly ground pepper
A few drops hot red pepper sauce

1 pound jumbo lump crabmeat

Lettuce leaves

1. In a small bowl, mix together all the sauce ingredients.
2. Carefully pick over the crabmeat to remove any bits of cartilage, but try to leave the crab in as large pieces as possible. Place the crab in a deep bowl.
3. Spoon the sauce over the crab and gently mix, breaking up the meat as little as possible. Let stand for at least 15 minutes.
4. Arrange lettuce leaves on serving plates and mound the crab salad in the center.

Serves 4 as a main course; 6 as a first course.

Fruity Flounder Salad

This refreshing and colorful salad is a boon for salad-lovers since it is best in the wintertime, when oranges are at their peak and most fruits a pale shadow of themselves. Dieters will appreciate the fact that the sauce contains no oil at all.

Each of the various ingredients can be prepared and refrigerated ahead of time. Assemble just before serving.

PREPARATION TIME   20 minutes

COOKING   15 minutes

1½ cups orange juice
6 slices fresh ginger
½ to ¾ pound flounder, sole, or
   cod fillet
¼ cup dry white wine
1 teaspoon cornstarch
2 tablespoons cold water
½ tablespoon butter or margarine

1 very ripe plantain*
1 orange
2 cups shredded lettuce
½ red pepper, cut into thin strips
1 tablespoon chopped fresh
   cilantro, or ½ tablespoon
   chopped fresh mint

1. Bring the orange juice and 5 slices of the ginger to the boiling point in a 6-cup nonreactive saucepot. Cover, reduce the heat, and simmer for 5 minutes. Meanwhile, diagonally cut the fish into slices about ½-inch wide and 4 inches long. Add the fish to the simmering juice, cover, and cook over very low heat for 3 minutes. Stir gently 2 or 3 times. If the fish is not cooked, remove from the heat and let stand in the hot liquid until the pieces are cooked through. Lift the fish out of the pot with a skimmer and transfer to a bowl. Discard ginger slices.
2. Peel and mince the remaining slice of ginger and add to the orange juice with the wine. Cook, uncovered, over high heat to reduce the liquid to about ¾ cup, approximately 5 minutes. Meanwhile, stir together the cornstarch and cold water, add to the simmering juice, and cook over medium heat for a minute or so, just until the sauce thickens a little and takes on a slightly transparent appearance. Spoon into a bowl and cool.

3. Peel the plantain and pull off all the fibrous strings; cut into ¼-inch slices. Heat a 12-inch nonstick skillet and add the butter or margarine. Spread the melted butter over the pan with a paper towel. Add the plantain slices and fry for a minute or so, until lightly browned. Turn and brown the other side. Remove from the skillet.

4. Prepare the orange by slicing off the ends. With vertical strokes, cut away the skin and white pith. Cut the orange in half vertically, then slice each half-section into ¼-inch half moon slices. If a small cutting board is used, retrieve the juices by scraping them into the sauce.

5. Make a bed of the shredded lettuce on a platter. Arrange a layer of the plantain over the lettuce and spoon about one-third of the sauce over the slices. Mound the fish in the center and alternate the orange and red pepper slices around the fish. Spoon the remaining sauce over the fish and sprinkle with the cilantro or mint.

Serves 4.

*Plantains are vegetable bananas, suitable for cooking and eating at just about every stage in their development. They are quite different from the dessert bananas commonly found in American markets. When green to yellow, plantains have little flavor and are prepared and used as a starch ingredient, similar to a potato. They ripen slowly at room temperature and can be refrigerated when they have matured to the desired degree. They will keep for several weeks. Plantains are ripe when they turn from brown to black, when they become slightly sweet and take on a banana aroma. Look for them in the fruit sections of many supermarkets or in Latin-American *bodegas* or markets.

Grilled Scallop and Corn Salad

The natural sweetness of corn plays against the briny-clean flavor of scallops, uniting them into a salad of delightful subtlety. Tomatillos add a mildly sharp accent and a lemony herbal flavor. This unique salad is best appreciated when warm, or at room temperature, so, if refrigerated, remove at least one-half hour in advance of serving.

PREPARATION TIME   5 minutes (10 minutes if using fresh corn)
COOKING   4 minutes
MARINATING   15 minutes

Vinaigrette

⅓ cup oil
1 tablespoon walnut oil
1½ tablespoons mild red or white
   wine vinegar
Salt and pepper

¼ teaspoon tarragon, chopped if
   fresh, crushed if dry
1½ tablespoons chopped fresh
   parsley

4 cups corn kernels, either frozen
   or cut from 4 large fresh ears
½ pound sea scallops

2 tomatillos, diced (page 35)
Salt and pepper
Romaine or radicchio leaves

1. To make vinaigrette, whisk all the ingredients in a bowl or shake them in a covered jar. Pour half the vinaigrette into a mixing bowl.
2. Cook the corn until it is tender, about 2 or 3 minutes, depending on its maturity. The kernels can be boiled in water or steamed. Drain thoroughly, shaking the strainer to eliminate excess water. Put the corn in the bowl with the vinaigrette and mix well. Use 2 wooden spoons, so as not to crush the corn. Cover and put aside for 15 minutes.
3. Pat the scallops dry on paper towels, then cut each in half horizontally. Heat a heavy nonstick skillet; if using a regular skillet, wipe it first with oil. Once the skillet is hot, quickly sear the scallops on both sides, about 15 seconds per side. Sprinkle with salt and pepper and add to the corn. Add the remaining vinaigrette and gently mix again.
4. Sprinkle the tomatillos over the salad and toss.
5. Line 4 salad plates with the lettuce or radicchio leaves. Mound the salad in the center.

Serves 4.

Warm Tuna and Leek Salad

Warm salads mean a little last-minute work, in this case a matter of minutes. Your reward is a more savory dish since chilling tends to diminish flavors and aromas.

The leeks can be cooked in advance, but leave a few tablespoons of liquid in the pan so you can thoroughly reheat them at serving time. Cover them tightly with plastic wrap if you store them in the refrigerator.

PREPARATION TIME   18 minutes
CHILLING   30 minutes
COOKING   20 minutes

¾ pound tuna steak, preferably in	½ cup dry white wine
1 piece	1¼ cups water
6 leeks	½ teaspoon dried thyme
2 tablespoons olive oil	Pepper

Vinaigrette

1 lime	Lettuce
6 tablespoons walnut oil, or	¼ cup chopped pimiento
extra-virgin olive oil	4 cherry tomatoes, halved
¼ teaspoon ground cumin	(optional)
Salt and pepper	4 parsley sprigs (optional)

1. Tightly cover the tuna steak with plastic wrap and place in the freezer for about 30 minutes.
2. Meanwhile, trim root ends of the leeks and cut off the dark green tops to about 1 inch above the white part. Make a cross cut into the light green tops to spread open the leaves that often trap sand. Rinse very well under cold running water to wash away any trace of sand and grit, then cut into 2-inch lengths. Cut each piece in half, lengthwise, then cut into thin julienne strips. Put all the leeks into a deep nonreactive skillet, add the olive oil, white wine, water, thyme, and pepper. Bring to a boil, cover, and simmer for about 10 minutes, or until the leeks are

soft. Remove the cover, turn up the heat, and boil briskly to evaporate the remaining liquid, about 4 minutes.

3. While the leeks are cooking, prepare the vinaigrette. Grate the zest from the lime and put into a small bowl. Squeeze juice from the lime and add to the bowl along with the oil, cumin, and salt and pepper. Whisk together very well. Shred the lettuce and place on 4 salad plates.

4. Remove the tuna from the freezer; it should now be firm enough to slice very thin. Heat a nonstick skillet until quite hot. If using a regular skillet, wipe it with oil. Place about one-third of the thin tuna slices into the hot skillet. Do not crowd the slices; they should sear quickly. Turn after about 5 seconds and sear the other side for an additional 5 seconds. Remove the cooked tuna slices to a dish and repeat with the remaining fish.

5. In the skillet, briefly heat the leek julienne. Mix in the tuna and the pimiento, Divide the warm salad among the 4 prepared salad plates and drizzle 2 tablespoons of the vinaigrette over each. Garnish with 2 cherry tomato halves and a parsley sprig.

Serves 4.

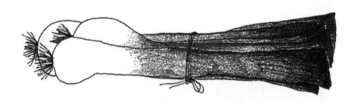

Lentil and Orange Roughy Salad

Lentils possess a wonderfully nutty flavor and need very little cooking time. Here the dull brown of the lentils is brightened by the addition of red pepper. Delicate finger-sized strips of snowy white fish crowns this unusual salad.

The lentil salad can be completely prepared in advance and refrigerated; bring to room temperature before cooking the fish.

PREPARATION TIME   18 minutes
COOKING   25 minutes
MARINATING   1 hour

2 cups uncooked lentils
1 medium onion, halved
4 whole cloves
1 carrot, quartered lengthwise and
   sliced
2 cloves garlic, peeled and minced

Salt and pepper
1 red pepper, peeled (page 34)
1 pound orange roughy fillet, or
   sole, flounder, or cod
Lettuce leaves

Dressing

¼ cup olive oil
¼ cup red wine vinegar
½ teaspoon curry powder
½ teaspoon ground ginger

½ teaspoon sugar
1 lemon
Salt and pepper

1. Rinse the lentils and put in a 2-quart pot. Press 2 cloves into each onion half and add to the lentils along with the carrot and garlic. Sprinkle lightly with salt and pepper and add enough water to cover the ingredients by about 2 inches. Bring the water to the simmering point, cover, reduce the heat, and cook for about 20 minutes, or until the lentils are just tender, but not soft and mushy.
2. Prepare the dressing in a large mixing bowl. Whisk together the olive oil, vinegar, curry powder, ginger, and sugar. Grate the lemon zest into the bowl, squeeze the juice from the lemon, and add it to the dressing. Add salt and pepper. Whisk the dressing thoroughly, taste,

and adjust the seasonings, if necessary. Pour half the dressing into a jar or pitcher and reserve.

3. As soon as the lentils are cooked, immediately remove the onion halves and drain the lentils and other vegetables. With a wooden spoon, press lightly on the lentil mixture to eliminate any excess water. Place the hot lentils in the bowl with the dressing, and toss quickly to coat thoroughly. Cover and put aside for at least 1 hour, mixing from time to time.

4. Cut the red pepper in half and pull out and discard the seeds and membranes. Slice 6 long, thin strips and reserve; cut the rest into small pieces and add to the lentils.

5. Rinse the fish fillet and pat dry. Feel for any bones and either pull them out or cut them away. Cut the fillet on the diagonal into long thin strips. Wipe a nonstick skillet with oil and place on high heat. Add the fish strips and cook quickly over high heat while turning them over constantly with a spatula. Depending on the texture and thickness of the strips, the cooking should take no longer than a few minutes. Sprinkle lightly with salt and pepper.

6. Taste the lentils and add more dressing, if desired. Spread out a few lettuce leaves on each of 6 plates. Spoon a thick layer of lentils over most of the lettuce and make a small mound of the fish strips in the center. Pour a little dressing over the fish. Cut the reserved pepper strips in half and crisscross them over the center of the fish. Serve warm or at room temperature and pass the remaining dressing separately.

Serves 6.

Oyster and Potato Salad

Shucked oysters are a boon to busy cooks. For most cooking purposes, standard size is best, and less expensive. If only very large oysters are available, cut them in half *after* they have been poached. This salad makes an attractive first course at dinner, or an excellent luncheon dish.

The oysters can be poached and the vinaigrette made the day before. It is best to cook the potatoes and string beans an hour or so before serving, so they can better absorb the vinaigrette.

PREPARATION TIME   18 minutes
COOKING   15 minutes

1 pint shucked oysters in their
  liquor

Poaching liquid

½ cup dry vermouth
⅓ cup olive oil
Juice of 2 lemons
2 bay leaves

½ celery rib
1 teaspoon light soy sauce
¼ teaspoon hot red pepper sauce
Salt and pepper

1 pound small red potatoes

Vinaigrette

3 tablespoons extra-virgin olive
  oil
2 tablespoons oil
2 tablespoons wine vinegar
½ teaspoon fresh basil

¼ teaspoon each dried rosemary,
  dried tarragon, and dry
  mustard
A dash hot red pepper sauce

¼ pound fresh string beans   · Lettuce leaves

1. Put the oysters and their liquor in a 4-cup nonreactive pot and add the poaching ingredients. Place the pot over medium heat and bring to a simmer. As soon as the liquid begins to bubble, remove pot from the

heat. Cover, cool, then refrigerate the oysters and the liquid until needed.

2. Scrub the potatoes and boil in a pan of boiling water to cover until tender, about 15 minutes to 20 minutes, depending on size. When cool enough to handle, peel and cut into ¼-inch slices. While the potatoes are boiling, prepare the vinaigrette in a jar and shake well. Put the sliced potatoes in a medium mixing bowl and pour the dressing over them. Mix gently with a wooden spoon to avoid breaking the slices. Cover and put aside.

3. Cook the string beans in boiling water until tender but still slightly crisp. Cool at once under cold running water. If time permits, cut them in half lengthwise and add to the potatoes.

4. About 15 minutes before serving, lift the oysters out of the poaching liquid with a skimmer and add to the potatoes and string beans. Lightly mix, then place on salad plates lined with lettuce leaves.

Serves 6 as first course, 4 as luncheon main course.

Tuna and White Bean Salad

This is a refined version of Italy's delicious *fagioli al tonna*, which uses canned tuna fish. That, too, is a good dish, but it lacks the finesse and the more delicate texture and flavor of fresh tuna.

You should allow time for the various flavors of this salad to mingle and mellow, so keep it in the refrigerator for a day, and remove about an hour before serving.

PREPARATION TIME   12 minutes
SOAKING   1 hour
COOKING   about 1 hour
MARINATING   1 hour

1¼ cups uncooked white pea
   beans
½ onion
1 whole clove
1 clove garlic, peeled and speared
   on a toothpick, plus ½ clove,
   peeled and cut into slivers

1 bay leaf
3 sprigs fresh basil
3 tablespoons olive oil
¾ pound tuna steak (without any
   dark sections)
¼ cup dry white wine
Salt and pepper

Vinaigrette

¼ cup extra-virgin olive oil
1 tablespoon balsamic or red wine
   vinegar
Salt and pepper

¼ cup diced red pepper
2 scallions, chopped
Lettuce or radicchio leaves
Capers (optional)

1. Rinse the beans, place them in a 2-quart pot, and cover with 2 inches of water. Bring to a boil, simmer for 2 minutes, remove from heat, cover, and let soak for 1 hour. The beans can also be soaked overnight in cold water.
2. Drain the beans, rinse out the pot, and return the beans to the pot. Cover with 2 inches of cold water. Stick the clove into the onion half and add it, along with the speared garlic, bay leaf, 1 basil sprig, and 1 tablespoon of the olive oil. Bring to a simmer and cook for about 1 hour, or until the beans are tender, but not mushy. (Do not boil too

rapidly; it tends to toughen the beans.) Add salt and pepper for the last 5 minutes of cooking.*

3. While the beans are cooking, cut little vertical and horizontal slits in the tuna steak and slip in the garlic slivers. Place in a heavy nonreactive pot, and add the white wine, the remaining 2 tablespoons olive oil and 2 basil sprigs, and salt and pepper to taste. Marinate for 15 to 30 minutes. Place the pot over medium heat and slowly bring the marinade to a simmer. Put a piece of aluminum foil directly over the tuna, cover with the lid, and cook gently for 7 to 10 minutes, depending on the thickness of the fish.

4. Combine the vinaigrette ingredients. Place the red pepper and scallions in a large mixing bowl.

5. Drain the beans and discard the onion, bay leaf, garlic, and basil. Add the hot beans to the bowl containing the red pepper and scallions. Pour the vinaigrette over and mix gently with a wooden spoon (do not mash the beans). Cover and put aside for 5 minutes.

6. Flake the cooked tuna into rough pieces. Add the tuna to the beans, along with ¼ cup of the marinade. Taste and add more marinade if needed; correct seasonings. Cover, and put aside to marinate for at least 1 hour, mixing occasionally.

7. Arrange lettuce leaves on salad plates, mound some of the fish and bean salad in the center, and garnish with capers, if desired.

Serves 5 or 6.

---

*When cooking beans, do not add salt to the water too early in the cooking process—it toughens the beans.

The Microwaved Catch

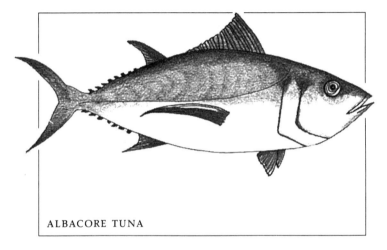

ALBACORE TUNA

Seafood and the microwave oven were made for each
other—fish cooked in this fashion retains
its juiciness, cooks evenly, and remains
moist and tender.

As we all know, the speedy cooking ability of the
microwave oven is a great boon to the busy cook. All
you have to do is arrange the fish, with a few
garnishes and seasonings, on an appropriate plate,
cover with a plastic wrap, and put into the microwave
oven. No pots or skillets to wash. It's an ideal
method for someone who wants to serve one or two
people quickly, with a minimum of fuss and bother.

A 700-watt full-size microwave oven was used in

developing these recipes. Smaller ovens may need more cooking time, although it's best to undercook the fish a little since it continues to cook for a short while once out of the oven. Keep in mind, too, that the strength of some herbs and spices diminishes in microwave cooking. You'll have to experiment to find the right formula for your oven and your tastebuds.

A word of caution about the plastic wrap covering. Use good-quality plastic wrap, made for microwave cooking. Puncture the wrap once (with the tines of a fork) before putting the dish into the oven, so excess steam can escape. And, once you remove the plate from the oven, slash the plastic at the side of the plate *away* from you, so you do not risk a steam burn.

Dilled Trout with Lemon

Depending on the rest of the menu, a single trout will serve two people. This uniquely flavored dish is practically foolproof.

PREPARATION TIME 5 minutes
COOKING 4 minutes

1 rainbow trout, ¾ to 1 pound, head removed
Salt and pepper
3 or 4 sprigs fresh dill or ½ teaspoon dried

1 lemon, thinly sliced
1 teaspoon olive oil
½ teaspoon anise-flavored liqueur
1 tablespoon dry white wine

1. Rinse and dry the trout, then lightly sprinkle the cavity with salt and pepper. Tuck the dill sprigs and about one-third of the lemon slices inside. Lay the fish in a microwave-safe dish and spread the oil over the top.
2. Place the rest of the lemon slices over the top of the trout. Mix the liqueur and wine together and pour over the fish. Cover with plastic wrap and cook at 100% power for 4 minutes.
3. Remove from the oven. The fish should be opaque. If not, return to the oven for an additional 30 seconds. When done, slash the plastic wrap on the side away from you and let the trout rest for 2 minutes before serving.

Serves 2.

Perch à la Basquaise

This is a spicy, hot dish, and its flavors are emphatic enough so that you can also serve it cold with a squeeze of fresh lemon juice. Slip a lettuce leaf underneath for a fresh green effect.

PREPARATION TIME 6 minutes

COOKING 7 minutes

4 scallions, chopped
1 cup chopped green pepper
1 cup chopped red pepper
1 tablespoon olive oil
¼ cup orange juice

Salt and pepper
¼ cup black olive slivers*
2 tablespoons fresh lemon juice
1 pound perch fillets, cut on the
    diagonal, in half

1. Put the scallions and both chopped peppers in a microwave pie plate or similar dish. Sprinkle on the olive oil, orange juice, and a little salt and pepper. Cover tightly with plastic wrap and microwave at 100% power for 3 minutes.
2. Put the vegetables in a bowl, add the olive slivers and lemon juice, and mix. Put the perch fillets in the pie plate, skin side down, and sprinkle lightly with salt and pepper. Spoon the vegetable sauce over the top. Cover with plastic wrap and microwave at 100% power for 2 minutes. Puncture the plastic wrap and let stand 2 to 3 minutes more to finish cooking.

Serves 4.

*Olives add a piquant flavor to a dish. It is preferable to buy fresh whole olives, and slice them, rather than the prechopped olive bits in a jar or the dull canned variety. In fact, you can vary the flavor of this and other dishes by experimenting with different kinds of fresh olives.

Monkfish with Mustard Sauce

Monkfish works best here because of its dense texture. If necessary, grouper, tilefish, or striped bass could be substituted. Do not use a grainy mustard in the sauce; its flavorings become too sharp when cooked. For extra color, steam broccoli florets to accompany the fish, and dress them with a mild vinaigrette to which chopped pimientos have been added.

PREPARATION TIME   3 minutes
COOKING   2½ minutes

Oil
Two 4-ounce monkfish fillets
1 teaspoon mild Dijon-style
  mustard
1 teaspoon oil

1 teaspoon light cream or half-
  and-half
⅛ teaspoon brandy
1 teaspoon bread crumbs
2 lemon wedges

1. Oil a 6- to 8-inch microwave-safe plate. Place the monkfish on the plate, and, if these are the tail pieces, tuck the tail end back against the body of the fish.
2. In a cup, mix the mustard, oil, cream, and brandy. Stir in the bread crumbs. Spoon the topping onto the fish and spread it over the entire surface. Do not cover with plastic wrap.
3. Cook at 75% power for 1½ minutes. Let stand for a minute and check for doneness. If necessary, cook for another 10 to 15 seconds. Timing will depend on the thickness of the fish. Transfer to serving plates and spoon the juices in the plate over the monkfish; add a lemon wedge to each plate. Serve hot.

Serves 2.

Gingered Shrimp

This attractive first-course dish can be enjoyed hot or cold. If served hot, supply some chunky fresh bread to soak up the sauce. If served cold, arrange the shrimp on a bed of lettuce as an exotic salad.

PREPARATION TIME   10 minutes
MARINATING   15 minutes
COOKING   1½ minutes

½ pound medium shrimp peeled
  and deveined

Marinade

½ to 1 teaspoon finely chopped,
  fresh ginger, to taste
½ clove garlic, minced
¼ teaspoon curry powder

1 teaspoon light soy sauce
½ teaspoon rice wine vinegar or
  mild white wine vinegar
1 teaspoon oil

4 scallions, cut in half crosswise

1. Place the shrimp in a dish. In a small bowl, mix all the marinade ingredients and pour the mixture over the shrimp. Mix well and put aside to marinate for 15 minutes.
2. Arrange the shrimp around a plate in a single layer, tail inward. Scatter the scallions over the top. Cover tightly with plastic wrap and microwave on 100% power for 1½ minutes. Let stand for 1 minute, and if not completely cooked through, return to the oven for an additional 20 seconds.
3. Divide the cooked shrimp between 2 warm dishes. Spoon some of the warm marinade over them and scatter the scallions on top.

Serves 2.

Tuna and Sprouts

The versatile tuna can stand up to strong flavorings and works well with mild accompaniments. It does both in this appealing dish.

PREPARATION TIME 8 minutes
CHILLING 15 minutes
MARINATING 15 minutes
COOKING 2 minutes

¼ pound fresh tuna
½ teaspoon aromatic bitters
1 tablespoon orange juice
⅛ teaspoon ground cumin
¼ pound bean sprouts
½ teaspoon ground ginger

1½ tablespoons oil
Juice of ¼ lime (1 to 2 teaspoons)
Salt and pepper
¼ red pepper, cut into strips and
  then cut crosswise

1. Wrap the tuna tightly in plastic wrap and place in the freezer for at least 15 minutes to firm the flesh. Cut into very thin slices. Stir the bitters, orange juice, and cumin in a 4-cup mixing bowl. Add the tuna, mix well to coat, and put aside for 15 minutes.
2. Heap the bean sprouts in the center of a microwave-safe 12-inch plate. Stir the ginger, oil, lime juice, salt, and pepper in a cup. Pour this sauce over the sprouts and toss to distribute the sauce. Mound the sprouts in the center of the plate. Place 2 of the red pepper strips in a crisscross pattern in the center of the mound and scatter the remaining pepper around the edge of the plate.
3. Place a single layer of the tuna slices over the red pepper and pour onto the fish any marinade remaining in the bowl. Cover the plate tightly with plastic wrap. Cook on 100% power for 2 minutes; remove plastic wrap and allow to stand for 1 minute.

Serves 2.

New Wave Tuna Sandwich

Just toss a few extra snow peas around this pretty "sandwich," and you have a complete main course. Serve with a mixed green salad.

PREPARATION TIME   3 minutes

COOKING   2½ minutes

½ pound tuna steak in 1 piece
½ teaspoon light soy sauce
1 teaspoon olive oil
⅛ teaspoon dried dill
Salt and pepper

6 snow peas
2 or 3 thin slices mozzarella
  cheese (preferably part-skim
  milk)
2 lime wedges

1. Keep the tuna cold until ready to cut. Using a sharp knife, cut the tuna steak in half; usually this will produce 2 triangular pieces. Cut each triangle in half horizontally.
2. Rub the inside of the bottom piece with ¼ teaspoon of the soy sauce and ¼ teaspoon of the olive oil. Scatter on half the dill, then lightly sprinkle with salt and pepper. Place 3 snow peas at the wider edge of the fish so that half the pea is visible. Put half the mozzarella on the bottom two-thirds of the steak. Cover with the top piece of the steak and rub the surface with olive oil. Repeat with the other steak.
3. Place the steaks on a microwave dish, cover tightly with plastic wrap, and cook at 100% power for 2½ minutes. Remove, uncover, and let stand for 30 seconds. Serve each with a lime wedge.

Serves 2.

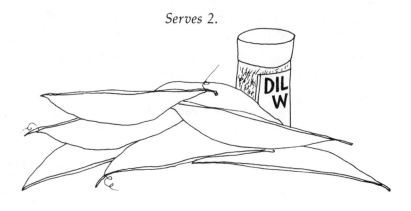

Index

Mussels, 2
  buying, 16
  cleaning, 17–18
  Cocktail, 56
  Moules à la Marinère (Steamed
    Mussels), 137
  Pizza, 179–80
  Provençale, 91–92
  Stuffed, 46
Mustard:
  -Glazed Pollock, 108
  Sauce, Monkfish with, 213

New Wave Tuna Sandwich, 216
Nutrition, 2–3

Oil, 24, 25–26
Omega-3 polyunsaturated fatty acids,
  2
One-Pot Clam Chowder, 93–94
Onion, Red, Sauce, Grouper with, 109
Orange Roughy Salad, Lentil and,
  203–4
Oriental Soft-Shell Crabs, 149–50
Oysters:
  Baked, 63
  buying, 16
  cleaning, 17
  Grilled, 49–50
  Herbed Scalloped, 64–65
  and Potato Salad, 205–6
  Soup, 86
  Spicy, 47–48

Papillotes, Fish Fillets in, 104
Parmesan, Scallops with, 55
Pasta, 156–66
  Fettuccine:
    with Mahimahi-and-Pepper Sauce,
      163–64
    with Tuna Sauce, 160
  Linguine with Clam Sauce, 158–59
  Penne with Smoked Fish Sauce,
    165–66
  with Swordfish Ragu, 161–62

Pastry, Russian Salmon Loaf in, 187–
  89
Penne with Smoked Fish Sauce, 165–
  66
Peppers:
  hot. See Hot Peppers
  red. See Red peppers
  yellow. See Yellow peppers
Perch:
  à la Basquaise, 212
  Simple Fish Sauté, 102
Pernod, Shrimp with, 45
Pesto, 32
Pie:
  Bluefish, 184–85
  Seafood, with a Potato Crust, 190–
    91
  Shrimp, in a Cornmeal Crust, 182–
    83
Pike, northern, 4
Pita, Monkfish and Sprouts in, 186
Pizza:
  Dough, 176
  Mussel, 179–80
  Shrimp and Spinach, 177–78
  Tuna and Vegetable, 181
Plaice, 7
Poached Red Snapper, 116–17
Poaching, 24
Pollock, 7
  Fisherman's Chowder, 97
  Mustard-Glazed, 108
  Seafood Pie with a Potato Crust,
    190–91
Potato(es):
  Crust, Seafood Pie with a, 190–91
  Green Goddess Scallop Soup, 84–85
  Salad, Oyster and, 205–6
  Smoked Haddock-Stuffed, 131–32
Pots and pans, 22, 167
Protein, 3, 19

Quick-Smoked Trout Canapés, 51–52

Ragu, Pasta with Swordfish, 161–62
Raw fish, 3